LONG JOURNEY FOR LOVE

LONG JOURNEY FOR LOVE

THE STORY OF PATRICK McBRIDE

ROSS GLOVER

CHAPTER 1

1921

The autumn of 1921 treated Patrick McBride with not only heartbreak at the death of his father, but also heartfelt joy on board RMS *Aquitania*.

Patrick McBride, the only son of Mary Ann and Shumate McBride, decided not to return to Princeton University to finish his senior year after his father died. His father, a Princeton alumnus, had insisted Patrick follow in his footsteps and study law at Princeton. Patrick had no interest in becoming a lawyer but wanted to study ancient history. However, to please his father, he attended Princeton on track for a law degree.

Patrick had no family in Kingsport, Tennessee. Aunts and uncles on both sides of the family died of Spanish flu in 1917 and 1918. His uncle Samuel, his only living relative, resided in Wichita County, Texas. and worked in the oil field at the Burkburnett Townsite. Patrick only saw him at family funerals.

Charles McMasters, his father's partner in the law firm and Mrs. Lydia McMasters were more family than his kin. When Patrick's mother died, it was Lydia McMasters who comforted him like an aunt. Now, she comforted him after his father died.

Whenever a prominent person died in Kingsport, after the funeral, friends and family gathered at the deceased's house for refreshment and sympathy. Lydia McMasters, standing in for Patrick, arranged and presided over the post-funeral event.

Patrick and his uncle Samuel accepted condolences from Schumate's friends. After everyone left, Patrick told his uncle, he had decided not to return to Princeton and wanted to travel around Europe for a year or so. Patrick declined his uncle's offer to go to West Texas with him and get a job in the oil fields. Patrick said he would consider the invitation when he returned from Europe. He booked passage on the HMS *Aquitania* to Liverpool, England and reserved a room in the Britannia Adelphi, the city's finest hotel, through a New York travel agent.

A week before Patrick sat out on his European journey, he and Charles McMasters sat at the kitchen table. Lydia McMasters made coffee.

"You're old enough to make your own decisions, and I respect your wishes,"Charles said. "Your Father was proud of you. Your grades were excellent, but I think he suspected you were not happy at Princeton. With your money, you can afford to travel. But you need to eventually settle down here in Kingsport."

"I went to Princeton for Dad's sake. I never wanted to be a lawyer. My interest lies in history. I'll use some money to travel in Europe for a year. Maybe, I when I come home, I'll return to college."

Lydia poured a cup of coffee and sat it in front of Charles. "Want a coffee?" she asked Patrick.

"No ma'am," Patrick said and nodded a negative. "Mr. McMasters, would you take care of my finances? I want to establish a Trust fund with two hundred thousand dollars I inherited and name yourself as Trustee. Dad kept seventy thousand dollars in Knoxville Savings and Trust. I'll take fifty thousand of that in cash and open a savings account in my name at the Knoxville Savings and Trust with thirty. When I get to Liverpool, I'll open a checking account at a bank there. I'll take a couple of thousand with me and arrange with a Liverpool bank to transfer money to the closest bank to where I am in Europe. Sell the house and keep the proceeds plus I'll sign my half of the building over to you as compensation for the work you do."

"Just as your Father told me, you're wise for your age. I agree to set up the trust and administer it. How much do you want to draw from the trust annually? Let me suggest five thousand and five hundred annually. That's better than the average salary of ninety percent of Americans."

"That's a good figure. I won't get married for a long time, but I'll need it when I do."

"If you budget and closely watch your spending, I will be surprised if you spend even a quarter of the twenty thousand. Write to me at least once a week and tell me where you are, so I'll know you are alive and well. Do not use any bank in Germany. By the time you exchange for German marks, inflation there will leave you with practically nothing."

On October 12, Patrick with Charles and Lydia McMasters waited at Kingsport station for the eastbound train to New York.

Lydia McMasters kissed his cheek and said goodbye with tears in her eyes. You be careful," Lydia McMasters warned him.

Charles McMaster echoed his wife's warning and said, "Don't forget to write."

CHAPTER 2

SHIPBOARD ROMANCE

Patrick McBride stood at the ship's rail on the stern of the RMS *Aquitania* and watched the skyline of New York City slowly shrink. The prospect of experiencing the culture of the old country suppressed his apprehension of the unknown. Most of his friends were in college or working. With twenty-five hundred passengers on board the ship, there was only a small chance of meeting an acquaintance.

At six feet tall and at a muscular weight of 185 pounds, he should be confident in himself. He wasn't. He set a goal to overcome his shyness, especially around girls, on this voyage.

In his three years at Princeton, he had two dates that ended in disaster. Lady's man Jack Terrill, was the first to entice him into a double date. Patrick's date only had eyes for Jack. He tried to hold her hand, which he thought was the natural thing to do, but she rebuffed him by whispering, "Keep away from me, creep."

The other date had a great personality, according to Patrick's friend Maxwell. She had a great deal of fat to go along with her personality and giggled through the whole affair. Patrick had become an excellent dancer after private lessons from Miss Landsdown in Kingsport. At dances he was the epitome of a male wallflower, standing back or sitting at a table watching. Due to his fear of rejection, he could never muster enough courage to ask a girl to dance.

Experienced travelers told him that by the time the ship reached port there were no strangers. He hoped that was true.

"Hello, young fellow," said an older man dressed in a tweed coat and sporting a cavalry mustache. "Are you traveling alone?"

"Yes, sir. I am."

"I'm Colonel Gadsden Formstone, late of the king's Shropshire Light Infantry. Do you dance, sir?"

"I do."

"Excellent. There is a dance tonight. A get-to-know-you-affair, informal, of course. I detest dancing, but my wife insists on our attending. I refuse to make a fool of myself, so I'm finding her a partner young enough to keep up with her. I do my best dancing while I sit with several gin and tonics and not move at all. Well, what do you think? Are you game enough? What is your name?"

"Patrick McBride. Why did you single me out?"

"You look rather lonely, and you're young."

"I had no plan to attend the dance, but now I have an excuse."

"I warn you, sir, you'll be on the dance floor all evening. Meet us at the bar tonight at eight. I'll introduce my wife," the colonel said.

Patrick had second thoughts about agreeing to dance with Mrs. Formstone. Blind dates always ended in disaster. Although not quite the same, it was a blind date. What if she turned out to be an ugly hag or a three hundred pound giggler. What would he do? He didn't care if Mrs. Formstone were sixty years old, tonight he wouldn't be a wallflower.

At ten minutes before eight, he entered the ballroom and looked for the bar. It was off to the left and Colonel Formstone signaled him to come over. A gorgeous blonde girl, apparently his daughter, stood next to the colonel. Patrick walked across the dance floor to the bar.

"Good evening, sir."

"Good evening to you, Patrick," the colonel said and took the girl's hand. "This is my wife, Elizabeth. Elizabeth, meet your dance partner for tonight, Mr. Patrick McBride."

Elizbeth Formstone's long, black gown, more formal than not, accented her slim figure. Gray eyes fit her long dark-blonde hair, a style that only she could wear and much more attractive than the way the American women bobbed their hair. Her smile captured and held Patrick so long; he came out of the enchantment only after she spoke. "Hello, Mr. McBride," she said. Her voice put temple bells to shame.

"My pleasure, ma'am. I hope you will not be disappointed," he said, and immediately thought what a stupid thing to say.

"Gaddy always picks excellent partners. Most are not as young as you."

"Colonel Formstone said he wanted someone young enough to keep up with you. I'm positive that's why he chose me. I hope I can live up to his expectations."

"The band will begin in about ten minutes," the colonel said. "You two find a table, and I'll be along shortly. I must speak to an old chum."

Elizabeth chose a table two rows back from the dance floor. She sat and invited Patrick to sit beside her by patting the chair.

"What is your story, Mr. McBride? Are you running away *from* something or *to* something?" she asked.

"Why do you ask, Mrs. Formstone?"

"Let's get these formal names out of the way. Call me Beth."

"And I am Patrick. Not formal, just my name."

"Very well, Patrick. Gaddy said that you're traveling alone. Everyone has a story. Tell me."

"Not much to tell, My dad died last month. I decided not to finish my senior year at Princeton. Instead, I search for something that I'll find or not find in Europe."

"I assumed you were running away from a love affair gone wrong. That is usually why a handsome man travels alone."

"Lady, I've had two dates in the past three years. Both turned out badly. I cannot lose my shyness. I get tongue-tied when I speak to a girl," Patrick told her.

"You're haven't been shy with me. Why is that?" Beth asked with an unforgettable smile.

"I can't say. You're married. That's as good a reason as any. And another, you put me at ease."

"If I were not married?"

"If you weren't married, normally, I would be tongue-tied. I get that way before beautiful girls. You are different. I cannot explain why I'm not stuttering over the shock of your beauty. As I said, you put me at ease when I first looked at you."

Beth smiled her enchantment.

"You two talking dancing the rabbit hop or whatever it is you do?" Colonel Formstone asked after he sat down across from Beth.

"We became better acquainted and used our given names. Patrick said his name is Patrick, so that's what we'll call him."

"I believe I'll call you 'colonel.' That matches your status," Patrick said.

"Good show. You'll fit in quite well," the colonel said.

As always, the orchestra began with a waltz for the older dancers.

"Colonel, will you dance the first dance with your wife?" Patrick asked.

"Patrick, I don't think you understand, I hate to dance, and I will not. You and Beth are the dancers. I do my best dancing with a gin and tonic here." He motioned at a glass of clear liquid.

"Mrs. Formstone, may I have this dance?" Patrick asked and gave her his hand.

"Of course, sir."

He took her in his arms, and her soft body, snuggled against his chest, felt as if it belonged there, and he had danced with her for years. The feeling unnerved him. The orchestra played a slow waltz.

"I've never heard that waltz. Do you know what it is?"

"It's the 'Glover's Ballad Waltz.' Rather obscure, but a happy tune," said Patrick.

"How do you know all this?"

"I have an exceptional memory. It'll be years before I forget this dance, if ever," Patrick couldn't believe he said that to her.

"I will be disappointed if you do forget."

The waltz ended. Beth and Patrick stood on the dance floor, waiting for the next waltz, which came, and they danced the next and the next. He held her closer with each waltz.

"I need some water," Patrick said.

"Very well."

He took her arm and walked across the floor to where the colonel sat.

"Colonel, is this water or gin?" Patrick pointed to a pitcher with clear liquid.

"It's water, old boy. Getting hot on the floor, eh?"

"Yes, a bit." Beth poured water into a glass and handed it to Patrick.

"Better go easy on poor Patrick. He'll have to last until the wee hours."

"I'll crawl to my cabin long before the wee hours, colonel."

Beth pouted.

"Good luck, my boy."

After two fast waltzes and three fox-trots, Patrick was not tired but knew if he didn't pace himself, he would wilt. "Let's take a break," he told Beth.

"Okay."

At their table, Colonel Formstone had succumbed to gin and was too drunk to stand.

"He's out for the night. Let's get him to our cabin," Beth said and motioned for a ship's attendant.

"Can you carry the colonel to our cabin, please?"

"Of course, madame," he said and motioned for another attendant. The two men placed the colonel in a rolling chair.

"I'll go tuck him in," Beth said.

"Good night," Patrick said.

"It that all the dancing you can do?"

"I need a partner," he said and looked around.

"I'll be back shortly. You stay there, Patrick, and don't let another girl take you off." Beth was back in fifteen minutes. "Gaddy is asleep for the duration. He drinks too much."

"Pity. The colonel seems like a good sort."

"He is and quite wealthy."

"Would you like to sit for a few minutes and tell me your story?" he asked.

"No, I'd like to stroll the deck."

Beth and Patrick left the ballroom arm and arm, and walked onto the darkened deck. They could hear "Roses of Picardy" sung by a tenor.

"That's one of my favorite songs," Beth said.

"I guess we do have something in common. "Roses of Picardy" is my favorite song, also. It is a sad song with a happy ending. I always look for my rose," Patrick said and looked at Beth. *Maybe Beth Formstone is my rose.* He dismissed the thought, after all, they had met only three hours ago.

"Let's sit here, and you tell me your story." Patrick indicated two deck chairs.

"Let's." Beth took Patrick by the hand and guided him to a deck chair love-seat. Someone left a blanket there, and Beth unfolded and covered them with it.

"A German bomb killed my parents when I was fifteen, she said. "Edna Formstone kept me until the war ended in 1918. Edna died in 1919, a year after Gaddy came home from the war. Since they had no children, I became their surrogate daughter. I graduated from a private girl's school the year Edna died. I moved back to the Formstone cottage and became Gaddy's housekeeper. He cooked up the plot to marry two years ago. It was his idea. His fortune will be fought over by relatives. As his wife, I inherit all, and they cannot touch it. He trusts me to distribute his money to his causes." She paused. "The rub in this plot is to be his true wife; we have to consummate the marriage. Poor Gaddy can't do that."

"I'm sorry. How can the relatives prove otherwise?"

"He sometimes talks when he's drunk. And if a friend of the relatives ever gets him alone and drunk, he'll probably tell," Beth said.

"He could live many years. Maybe outlive the relatives."

"No. This trip is our last transatlantic crossing. Gaddy is very sick with cancer in his stomach. He has not long to live."

"Does the gin not aggravate the colonel's condition?" Patrick asked.

"He enjoys gin and tonic; he will not give it up. He claims and rightly so, it won't kill him."

"Will doctors prescribe morphine?"

"He is an old soldier and thinks he should set an example for other suffering veterans. He refuses to take morphine," Beth said. "But the pain hasn't been that bad lately."

"He is rather jolly to be dying. It must be awful for you. I wish there were something I could do."

Beth took Patrick's arm and turned him to face her. "Patrick, you've helped this night more than you know. I've not been with anyone my age for a long time because we don't want the relatives to think I'm not loyal to the marriage. Here, in the middle of the Atlantic, no one will see us or even care. The way you held me was more than a thrill," she said and kissed him full on the lips.

He returned her long, caring kiss, the first he had since ninth grade when Sue Hampton grabbed and kissed him.

"Beth, you are a special lady. I am not shy with you and forever grateful for proving that I can talk to girls without stuttering. But there is something else that I cannot explain. The orchestra is still going strong. Are you ready to go back for another fox-trot?"

"It's such a lovely night. Let's sit and enjoy the stars." They listened to the combo playing "Roses of Picardy" by request and tightly held each other as if they would never see the other again. They forgot about dancing and reluctantly released each other in the wee hours of the morning.

At her cabin door, Patrick told Beth, "Although I've known you just hours, it seems I have known you forever. I would stay, on this ship, with you until the sea dries up and forever after."

"That's my feeling too," she replied.

Beth and Patrick were constantly together day and night for the remainder of the crossing. During the day they played shuffleboard and strolled the decks getting to know each other. They talked and laughed. At night after dinner, Beth sat in Patrick's lap in a deck chair, wrapped in a blanket, as they kissed and petted. One night Patrick became bold enough to ask, "Beth, would you object if I called you 'sweetheart,'—in private, of course?"

"If I have permission to call you 'darling,'" she answered.

"How could I deny you that, sweetheart."

"You're kind, my darling."

They didn't talk about the future, knowing it was impossible to plan because of circumstances with Gaddy. But while they didn't talk about the future with each other, it was in their thoughts. Each wanted to profess his or her love but held back knowing if they did, Beth would abandon her obligation to Colonel Formstone. Almost every night the orchestra played, and the tenor sang, "Roses of Picardy." They heard the song so many times, they memorized the lyrics and sang along with the tenor.

Colonel Formstone left them alone and only appeared at lunch and dinner. During their time together, Patrick asked the colonel to tell stories of his exploits in India and the war. It delighted the old soldier that someone listened and enjoyed his rambling. The colonel and Patrick became friends. The three dined together every night during the five days it took to reach Liverpool.

Each night Colonel Formstone drank his gin and tonic until he passed out. If he suspected anything, he said nothing until the night before docking at Liverpool. Beth, the colonel, and Patrick met to enjoy a formal dinner in the dining room on deck five.

"Beth, please have the stewart show you to our table, I want to speak privately with Patrick a minute," Colonel Formstone said and led Patrick to the sitting room at the side of dining room entrance.

"Patrick," he said, "you're a good lad. I appreciate the attention you've shown Beth. You two have been together too long to have secrets. So, you know I am not long for this world, and when I leave, I want Beth to take care of my affairs. I am quite wealthy, and I want my legacy to go where it will do good. And not to my greedy relatives. It shall be Beth's job to do what I request. We are married in name only. Unfortunately for me, I cannot consummate the marriage. Here I come to the hard part. I feel Beth wants to go with you. And I need her with me when I die. Therefore, I plead with you not to urge her to be with you. I have no right to dictate to you what you can or cannot do. But I ask as a new and admiring friend."

"Colonel, Beth has not hinted at going with me. If she did, I would be a sorry man to turn her down. But knowing your situation and what you want to do, I'd be even sorrier to agree to her wishes. Don't worry. Beth will be at your side when your day comes. We have not talked about being together, and I'm not sure how one knows if he is in love or not. If the deep feelings I have for her are love, then I love her with all my heart. Will you keep that to yourself? If Beth feels the same, I want her to tell me."

"You are a true gentleman. I shall have to find some way to show my appreciation," the colonel said.

At dinner, Colonel Formstone said, "Too bad you don't partake in strong drink, Patrick. I'll leave you two to your own devices and indulge in my great joy . . . gin and tonic. Beth, my dear, I'll have Charles take me to the cabin if I am incapacitated, and I hope to be that. Good night, Patrick. We'll have our goodbyes tomorrow."

"Sleep well, colonel."

"Good night, Gaddy," Beth kissed him on the cheek.

"Good night, dear."

That night, as was the custom, Beth and Patrick sat in a deck chair. He held her close and kissed her; she responded in kind. They talked about nothing and everything. When sleep finally caught up, Patrick escorted Beth to her cabin.

"My life is so complicated, and I must stay and carry out Gaddy's wishes. Promise me you'll not forget me, my darling." Beth said.

"And you me, my one and only sweetheart," Patrick said and they sealed their promises with a kiss.

The three disembarked the RMS *Aquitania* in Liverpool the next day and stayed together through customs.

"Where will you stay in Liverpool, Patrick?" Colonel Formstone asked.

"I'll stay at the Britannia Adelphi. I'll stay a week or so and explore the countryside. I want to see the first iron bridge over the Severn River at Telford. I'll catch a train to London and sightsee. I cannot tell you where I go from there. I'll be back in Liverpool next year to catch a steamer home. What is the date?"

"October twenty-second," Beth said.

"I will be back here on this date, October twenty-second, in one year at the Adelphi," Patrick said and looked at Beth to make sure she knew what he meant. She nodded.

"I hope to see you again. If you're up our way, come see us in Shrewsbury," Colonel Formstone said.

"Yes, sir. I will. And Beth, I cannot tell you how much I've enjoyed our dances. Thank you."

"At last, I finally found a dance partner that would keep me dancing. I thank you, Patrick," Beth said and stood on her tiptoes, and kissed him. She pressed into his hand a note. It wasn't her intention to let him go with just a note, but she could not let the situations get more complicated than they already were.

Beth watched him cross the street and turn to look at her. He gave her a smile and small wave of his hand. She felt faint and almost collapsed. Beth held back the urge to abandon all her promises to the colonel and run to him. She wanted to tell him how much she loved him. She wanted to scream," Wait, my darling, wait for me, I'm going with you."

She knew Gaddy had spoken with Patrick about his situation and didn't know what he would do. Her loyalty to Colonel Formstone won out.

At the Adelphi Hotel, Patrick opened Beth's note and read,

Please, never forget me. I want so much to see and be with you again. Come to Wems at 32 Oxford Street.

He folded the note with a sigh and put it in his inside coat pocket for safe keeping. Should he write to her? It sounded like she cared for him. *I won't write because one of the colonel's kin could intercept the letter and know of Beth's interest in another man.*

Patrick lost the note somewhere in Italy. He remembered Wem and Oxford but forgot the house number. It didn't mean he couldn't search for her. If she were in Wem, nothing would prevent him from finding her home.

CHAPTER 3

LETTERS FROM EUROPE

October 22, 1921
Liverpool
Dear Lydia and Mr. McMasters,

Arrived safely in Liverpool. The Aquitania passengers were great and I danced with a young lady my age. Beth Formstone and I were together all the way across. She is a delightful traveling companion. On my way to London, then to France.

Yours,

October 30, 1921
London
Dear Folks,

London is everything I imagined it to be. There is history on every corner, and I love it. Visited Westminster Abby and the infamous Tower. So much history in the British Museum, the Museum of London, and others I will tell you when I get home. Another few days here and then on to France.

Yours,

November 20, 1921
Dear Folks,

Took channel ferry across the channel to Cherbourg.

French people are friendly and grateful for America's help in the war. On to Verdun and Argonne Forest. French citizens and army are clearing battlefields of explosives. It will take years to get all dangerous war material out of these sites. Tourists are forbidden to enter battle sites except for cemeteries. Going to safer ancient historical sites.

Yours,

Patrick saw Beth everywhere. There were girls with the same hair and the same curvy body. He couldn't get here out of his mind no matter how hard he tried.

December 3, 1921
Dear Folks,

Chilly here. Peacoat comes in handy. Saw impressive Roman ruins at Reims. Only Gallic tribe to support Julius Caesar during wars with Gaul. Provence has more standing Roman ruins than anywhere I can even think of except Italy. In Nimes, Roman city with many standing Roman built square house. Will explore here for a while.

Yours,

December 21, 1921
Dear Folks,

The Dubois, a French family, invited me to Christmas dinner and to meet Father Christmas. Wonderful people. Will continue in Provence visiting Roman sites afterward. Unbelievably preserved Port du Gard aqueduct north of Nimes. Wish you were here to see these magnificent ruins. Could stay for years.

Yours,

January 1922
Dear Folks,

Visited Roman docks in Marseille. Alesia, where Caesar defeated the Gaul. Saw Agincourt battlefield. English King Henry V victory over French in Hundred

Years War. Not much to see, just muddy field. Remember Shakespeare's Henry V's Saint Crispin's Day speech. On to Paris.

Yours,

He left his hotel, strolled down the street, and began to think what would do when he next saw Beth. He saw a girl go into a café. It was Beth. It had to be. Her profile was Beth's. He rushed inside the Café Le Jardin Du Petit Palais and as he passed the two men standing at the bar he brushed against one who held a glass of wine. The wine splashed on the fellow's coat.

"Hold on, young fellow. Where are you going in such a hurry?"

Patrick stopped abruptly. "I'm sorry sir. May I buy you whatever it is you are drinking to make up for the spill?" he said still watching Beth as she sat down at a table with a couple. His heart fell when he saw it wasn't Beth.

"You're an American. I knew it the minute he came in," the other man said.

"My name is Fitzgerald, and this is Ernest Hemingway," the first man said, indicating the man with him. "Who are you and what or who are you looking for?"

"I'm Patrick McBride from Tennessee, and I followed that girl at the table with the couple. She looks like a girl I met coming over."

"Is she in Paris?"

"I don't know. Probably not. She's English."

"Ah, Women are bad, Whiskey is good," Hemingway said and hiccupped. "

"Do you work in France?" asked Fitzgerald.

"No. I am touring Europe for a year," Patrick said. "Do you work here, Mr. Fitzgerald."

"Yes and no. I'm a writer. Mostly short stories. I work wherever I want. Paris inspires me, and I get more done here. Hemingway works on a novel here," he said. "Will you have a glass of wine or something stronger?"

"No. I don't drink. Thanks for asking. I must be going. What is your first name? I'll look for some of your stories."

"Scott Fitzgerald. F. Scott Fitizgerald."

February 27, 1922
Dear Folks,

Fun in Paris. Lots of jazz bands. Witnessed cancan dance (not that risqué).

Walked Avenue des Champs-Elysees and a boat trip on Seine River. Nightclubs. Met two Americans in Cafe Le Jardin Du Petit Palais. A fellow named Hemingway, a writer in his cups, and Scott Fitzgerald, a short-story writer. Delicious food including (yuck) snails. Will stay in Paris for five weeks then on to Belgium.

Yours,

March 6, 1922
Dear Folks,

Very sad Flanders Field cemetery. The first battle of war, Battle of Liège. A lot of German casualties. Belgium still smarting from war. I saw trenches dug from one side of France to the other. Can't understand language here. On to Germany. Will write from there.

Yours,

March 19, 1922
Dear Folks.

Germany is politically devastated by the Great War. Germans are living for the day. Young people gather in clubs and drink the night away. I cannot see where they get money. Prostitution runs rampant in cities. The whole country is decadent and depressing. Not good at all. I do not like Germany. I'm leaving as soon as I see two sites.

Yours,

March 24, 1922
Dear Folks,

I have traveled on foot, on buses and trains. Today, I rode a Rhine Riverboat for thirty miles. Unbelievably beautiful river. It is my most memorable ride. The political talk is Germany has no gold to pay reparations.

I heard that the Deutschmark would soon be worthless. That, I can believe.

Yours,

March 30, 1922

Dear Folks,

Left Germany this morning on a train through Switzerland to San Marino, a small independent country on the northern border of Italy and Switzerland. If I could see all the Swiss Alps, I would. We stop for water and look, but that's about it. Maybe I'm tired, but if you have seen one mountain, you have seen them all.

Yours,

April 10, 1922

Dear Folks,

Surrounded by Italy, the small country of San Marino retains its independence. I can walk from one side of San Marino to the other in a couple of hours. Its walled city is one of the oldest and best preserved in all Europe. It is pure medieval and quite enjoyable. I'll be here for one day. Keep the envelope with the San Marino stamp.

Yours,

April 15, 1922

Dear Folks,

Finally, in Italy. Florence, Julius Caesar's city, is in the Tuscany region. It is rooted in Italian culture and history. Artists Botticelli, Paolo Uccello, Leonardo da Vinci, and Michelangelo have their creations in museums here. My history studies told me Florine bankers created the double-entry bookkeeping system. Italian history resides in Florence.

Yours,

Patrick wrote letters to the McMasters in the evening and dreamed about Beth at night.

May 12, 1922
Dear Folks,

I could never get tired of Rome. I saw the pope briefly when he blessed the crowds from the balcony. I loved Italy. People were friendly and helpful. I picked up a wee bit of Italian. Not hard when you have a dictionary. Visited the Coliseum. Went to Protestant Cemetery to visit the graves of Keats, Shelly and Navy Commander Thomas Jefferson Page. Captain Page served in U.S. Navy and Confederate Navy, and helped Italy develop a modern navy. The catacombs were spooky but exciting. I met Guido Marcellus, a Catholic university professor, who told me about an Italian politician, Benito Mussolini, who formed the National Fascist Party. Professor Marcellus said that he would be elected Prime Minister and that will be bad for Italy.

Yours,

June 6, 1922
Dear Folks,

Today, at Pompeii I stood in the shadow of Mount Vesuvius. Excavation still goes on and probably for many more years. There are lava-encased bodies. The day before yesterday on the 4th, I toured the Herculaneum ruins. Saw beautiful mosaics, preserved when mud flowed into the city. It will take many years to excavate Pompeii and Herculaneum fully. Lots to see and absorb.

Yours,

June 25, 1922
Dear Folks,

In Sicily. Here are ancient ruins of Greek and Roman civilizations. The Temple of Concord is exciting and beautiful. Greek theaters are all around. I favored the theater of Taormina. A spectacular theater built in the third century BC. You can sit in the seats and see Mt. Etna and the ocean. Pieces of a giant statue that is said to have held up a section of a temple are fantastic.

August 1, 1922
Dear Folks,

Going back to mainland Italy today. I will take a ship north to Venice. Will write from there.

Yours,

August 17, 1922
Dear Folks,

An interesting city here. Great architecture. One is the Patriarchal Cathedral Basilica of Saint Mark. Truly breath-taking. The palace of the Doge (?). Saw prisons, many rooms and almost got too tired to see any more.

Yours,

September 12, 1922
Dear Folks,

I didn't think I would ever tire of touring Italy, but I am. Going on to Lake District by train and hole up in Milan for a week or so. Then over the Alps and Paris. Later to London. I'll write when I get to England.

Yours,

Patrick counted the days when he would go to Shrewsbury. When he thought of Beth, his heart beat a little faster. He longed to see her and hold her in his arms.

CHAPTER 4

BETH STRUGGLES

Beth Formstone vividly remembered watching Patrick McBride walk away and then turn, smile and give a half wave. At that moment, Beth's love for him was so great that she almost fainted. She thought if it were possible to reverse time, Patrick McBride would never again walk away from her. The memory of Patrick's arms around her kept her going through the ordeal with the dying colonel and his niece and nephew looking on like carrion eaters. When she and Patrick meet in October, Beth will ask him to stay in Wem and marry her.

The colonel's niece and nephew who had not spoken to him in ten years began to inquire about his health. Someone had told them that he was dying of stomach cancer. Beatrice and Banny lived off their mother's money and had never worked a day in their lives. But their cash cow was drying up. They knew their uncle's cancer would soon take him and waited like vultures for him to die, so they could claim his wealth.

He thought of a scheme to keep his sister's children from getting anything. He set his plot in action when he married Beth in 1920 and named her sole beneficiary of his fortune. Colonel Formstone filed a document with Ralph Hawkins, his solicitor, with instructions how he wanted his wealth distributed and left nothing to his sister's boy and girl. Hawkins held the document for Beth. They never con-summated the marriage. If his niece and nephew found out, they could get the colonel's will nullified and become the beneficiaries. Colonel Gadsden Formstone, late of the King's Shropshire Light

Infantry, paid his debt to society August 7, 1922.

At Shrewsbury, the Copthorne Barracks turned out for a military funeral for Colonel Gadsden Hallock Formstone, DSO. and DSC. The daily newspaper described his funeral as an event the citizens of Shrewsbury would never again witness. Beth Formstone, his widow, tearfully watched the impressive ceremonies honoring their old colonel. His niece and nephew sat dry-eyed and glared at her.

Immediately after the brigade commander presented a Union Jack to Beth, Colonel Formstone's niece and nephew left, and kept their appointment with a local lawyer. Throughout the proceedings, Beth could not keep her thoughts from Patrick McBride.

An officer from the barracks took Beth back to her cottage in Wem where Mrs. Peploe and three other neighbor women waited with food and comfort. Beth braced herself for what was coming, the long and drawn-out legal battles over the will and her inheritance. The next morning, she spoke with her solicitor Ralph Hawkins, and asked the brigade commander William Bishop, who witnessed the signing of the will, for any help he could give.

What Beth expected happened two days after the funeral; the Bandons filed a caveat at the probate registry to challenge Gadsden H. Formstone's will. She couldn't probate the will until the probate court notified them of impending action, the notice that Beth filed to probate the will at priory courts in the Birmingham District Probate Registry on August 10th, 1922. The siblings' solicitor challenged the will on the grounds that Elizabeth, his wife, coerced him into leaving his fortune to her with no inheritance to his niece and nephew, his blood kin. They further claimed that his will should provide a sum of money for their upkeep.

Beth sat and listened to her co-executor solicitor, Ralph Hawkins, tell her what he expected to happen. She wished there was a way to contact Patrick to lean on through the situation. Beth prayed she could convince him to stay in Shrewsbury when they met in October.

A young man knocked softly on the solicitor's office door and came in. "Hello," he said.

"Mrs. Beth Formstone meet my associate, Philip Kelly. He will be working the case on your behalf. If you need anything, call Philip," Hawkins said.

"It is my pleasure, Mrs. Formstone. I look forward to our association," Philip Kelly said.

"And I look forward to resolving this situation as quickly as possible. Since we will see each other often, I suggest we drop the formality and go by given names. You may call me, Beth. I will address you as Philip if that is agreeable," Beth said and thought how handsome he was and compared him to Patrick. *My love is rugged, and Kelly looks soft.*

"Very well, Beth."

"What is our next move?" she asked. Or do we sit and wait them out?"

"Yes and no. As your solicitors, we have applied for a grant of representation at the registry in Birmingham. The caveat filed by Beatrice and Banny, her brother, prevents the court from issuing a grant of representation. It lasts for at least six months, but the two can stop probation as long as a year or more. If you and the niece and nephew cannot resolve the problem, the court will put your case on a court docket and send it to a jury to decide."

"That seems unfair to the colonel's wishes," Beth said.

"The judicial system works for both sides of a dispute. There are times when the caveat works for the benefit of the wronged party," said Hawkins and added, "Prepare for a long battle before we can probate his will. And if we win, it may take a year or so to sell all the colonel's assets and distribute per his instructions."

"Is there a way to prepare all paperwork to distribute the money according to his instructions before probating the will?"

"We cannot sell any of Formstone's assets, but I have a list of what he owns" Hawkins said. "He paid off all monetary obligations before he died. I'll look at Gadsden's instructions and have Philip Kelly, my associate, prepare paperwork. Philip will be in charge of handling the process now. He will work closely with you."

"You are named coexecutor, can't you still be involved?"

"I will, Mrs. Formstone. But Kelly will be my legs," Hawkins said.

Formstone had left instructions with Hawkins on how to dispose of this fortune in case something happened to Beth.

"I must warn you; we will go through many twists and turns to get the will probated" Hawkins said. "To start, I want Philip Kelly to take you to court in Birmingham for two days. We will attempt to rush things along, and you'll get a feel for what you are to go through with the disputed will. While you are there, it would not hurt to make some friends at the registry. Sometimes insiders can tell you what is happening in your case before your lawyer."

Beth and Philip Kelly traveled to Birmingham several times to speed up the process. They took a train back to Shrewsbury and Kelly escorted her home in his car. Mrs. Peploe saw them often and thought they made a lovely couple.

Lawyers Ralph Hawkins and Philip Kelly thought they had a breakthrough when the Bandons' lawyer called to set up a meeting in Birmingham.

Hawkins told Beth about the meeting. "You have been as close to the case as Kelly and myself. We want you to go in case we need a decision to accept or not their proposal. We leave tomorrow on the morning train."

"This is October nineteenth. I have to be in Liverpool on Sunday, October twenty-second without fail," Beth said.

"Stay at the hotel Saturday night. You'll need the rest after our meeting. We'll see you catch the early train," Philip Kelly told her.

Hawkins, Kelly, and Beth silently waited in the registry conference room for Beatrice, Banny and Benjamin Cole, their lawyer, to arrive. After thirty minutes, Cole came into the conference room followed by the Bandons.

"Get that whore out of here. We didn't agree to her presence," Banny said.

"What are you trying to do, Cole. Bring us together like one happy family?" screamed Beatrice. "We'll not confer while she is still here."

"Well, obviously, you are not ready to negotiate. Let the courts sort it out," Hawkins said. He gathered his notebook and papers and slid them into his briefcase.

"Wait," Cole said. "We can work something out."

"Like hell, we will," Banny said. "When we're through with that prostitute," Banny said, pointing to Beth, "she'll be begging on the street."

"Mr. Cole, explain to your client what defamation of character is. Good day, sir," Hawkins said.

Beth, Kelly, and Hawkins sat in a small tea room across from the registry and discussed what had happened.

"They are crazy or just greedy. Probably both," Kelly said

"I predict the Bandons will hold out until they're short of money. If we hold our own and let them make the first move, I think we can get our way with minimal cost," said Hawkins.

That night Beth slept lightly, rehearsing what she would say to Patrick. *How do I approach him? I know he cares for me and even loves me. How stupid we were for not admitting our love for another. We came close so many times on the* Aquitania.

She decided to grab and hug him and say over and over again "I love you."

Chapter 5

Before Parting "Say I Love You"

Patrick left London and traveled north with short stops at Bath, Stonehenge, Stratford-upon-Avon and Liverpool. It was October eighteenth when he checked into the Britannia Adelphi and decided to rest two days while hotel laundry cleaned his clothes. Thinking of Beth, the young man slept fitfully that night.

Early that morning he knew he could not wait three days for her to come to Liverpool on the twenty-second. He longed for her so deeply and felt he would die if he didn't hold her and tell of his love. Patrick dressed, packed his clean clothes in the beat-up valise, and checked out of the Britannia Adelphi.

He bought a through ticket on the first train to Shrewsbury. Although he lost the note with her address on it, Patrick remembered Oxford Street in Wem.

On the train to Shrewsbury, he sat facing an older lady and girl about the same age as Beth. After the train left the station, curiosity got the better of the girl.

"Are you going all the way to Shrewsbury?" she asked.

"Yes, I am."

"I overheard you at the ticket window. Are you from Canada?"

"I from the United States, state of Tennessee."

"We don't meet too many Americans here. Are you here on business?"

"No. I am going to see a lady and ask her if she loves me," Patrick said.

"How exciting. What is her name? I may know her," the girl asked.

"Beth Formstone. She lives in Wem."

"Too bad. I wouldn't know Beth Formstone. I've lived in Dorrington all my life, and I've never been to Wem because it is a distance from where I live. You must love her very much to come all this way."

"I do. Beth Formstone is the only girl I ever loved."

When they exited the train at Dorrington, the girl said, "Luck to you. I hope the lady loves you, and you both will be happy."

He arrived after dark that afternoon and booked a room at the Shrewsbury Hotel, a few minutes walk from town center.

He settled in the hotel room and decided to begin his search for Beth Formstone the next day. He nervously sat in his room and fantasized about surprising Beth.

Patrick slept restlessly, and he dreamed of Beth. He held her in his arms and told her how much he loved her. The young man woke up early the next morning and hurriedly dressed. He ate in the hotel dining room on an egg and two pieces of streaky bacon. Patrick left on the nine o'clock morning train to Wem. He was there in fifteen minutes. He inquired about Colonel Formstone from a constable.

"I knew the old colonel. He was a good man, even if he fancied gin and tonic more than he should. The colonel left this earth some three months ago. Beth, whom he married, is the young woman that kept house," the constable said and paused. "Folks said for his money. I don't believe everything I hear. He wasn't senile and knew what he was doing when he married a woman young enough to be his daughter. His estate is tied up with litigation and Mrs. Formstone has a battle on her hands. The colonel's nephew and niece are trying to have the civil action transferred to a London court. It could take years to resolve. Mrs. Formstone has gone for a month now. With all the litigation, she spends a lot of time with Mr. Philip Kelly; I'm sure he supports her through the traumatic times."

"Can you direct me to the Formstone house?"

"Yes. There's no one at home so that it may be a useless trip. The house is on Oxford Street. Walk about four blocks down High Street and turn on Oxford. It is the third cottage on the left," the constable told him.

Patrick found the Formstone cottage. He knocked on the door, but no one came, and he heard no movement in the house. Mrs.

Peploe, the next-door neighbor, called to him.

"Young man," she said. "Ye'll find no one there. Colonel Formstone died these past months, and Mrs. Formstone is in Birmingham with Mr. Kelly. Colonel Formstone's kin are attempting to get his fortune, and Beth, Mrs. Formstone, says there will be a long battle in the courts. I am to take care of the house in her absence. It will be a long time before she comes back."

"Who is Mr. Kelly?"

"He is one of her solicitors, and I can see he is a little more than just a solicitor. They look like they belong together. Lovely couple."

"My name is Patrick McBride. I met the colonel and Beth on the *Aquitania* coming over. The colonel was a good man. I enjoyed his company and liked him very much. Please give my sympathy to Mrs. Formstone. I'm glad she found someone to support her." Patrick said. "I'm sorry I didn't see her before the colonel passed." Patrick's heart fell, and a great sadness came over him.

He took a page from his notebook and wrote, "I love you Beth and could not wait in Liverpool to see you. I will never forget you. And I hope you'll have a happy life with Mr. Kelly."

Intentionally, he didn't include an address. He folded the note and slipped it under her door. Patrick knew Beth wouldn't give up the fight for what the colonel wanted to be done with his wealth. He admired her for her tenacity and hoped that Mr. Kelly loved her as much as he did. The note told her their time together was not a shipboard romance for he had fallen deeply in love and regretted not telling her. He was sorry that she didn't feel the same about him.

Mrs. Peploe saw the sadness and thought it was for Colonel Formstone. "Don't feel sad for the colonel, he is with God and sings with the angels in Heaven."

With a tear in his eye, the young man turned and bid farewell to Mrs. Peploe.

Patrick took the train from Wem back to Shrewsbury and the next train to Liverpool. He checked into the Adelphi. Now, there was no reason to stay in England. The following day at the docks he inquired about any ship sailing for the United States and a shipping clerk directed him to a list of ships, coming and going from Liverpool, posted on a bulletin board. On the list was a freighter leaving the next day, bound for Savannah, Georgia. He booked a cabin on the *Bristol Star* and sailed early on the morning of October twenty-second.

Beth Formstone stored her bags at the Liverpool train station and walked almost at a run to the Britannia Adelphi. Out of breath, she impatiently waited at the desk for a clerk.

"May I help you?" the desk clerk asked.

"Please tell Mr. Patrick McBride that Beth Formstone is waiting for him in the lobby. He is expecting me."

"Mr. McBride? He checked out early this morning. I'm sorry you missed him."

"Did he say where he was going."

"He came back from Shrewsbury. I'm sorry he didn't say."

"Did he say if he will be back?"

"He did not."

Tears welled in her eyes. "He was supposed to be here on the twenty-second. Maybe he'll still be in Wem when I get home." She wrote him a note telling him to come back to Wem and that she loved him. She gave the letter to the concierge to put in Patrick's mailbox.

The day after Patrick sailed, the Adelphi concierge looked in Patrick's mailbox and saw the note he failed to get. He remembered the lovely young lady that left it. He read the letter: "Come back to Wem. I'll be waiting. I will never forget you. I love you."

Maybe she caught up with him, after all, thought the concierge and crumbled the paper before tossing it into the trash container.

Beth found Patrick's note when she opened the door of the house on Oxford Street. She read the letter and tears fell on the paper in her hand as she read it once more.

Mrs. Peploe called to her, "Beth, a nice young man came by the day before yesterday to see the colonel. His name is Patrick McBride and said to give you sympathy. Please don't cry; your troubles will be over before you know it."

"No, Mrs. Peploe, I think not. I have lost a man I deeply love and don't know how it happened. I may never get him back," Beth said sobbing, when she entered her house.

CHAPTER 6

PATRICK'S TRIP HOME

On the *Bristol Star,* Patrick didn't find the lap of luxury. He ate with the crew. Most were Brits, who could tell he had money and didn't understand why he chose a slow freighter to return to America. Most passenger ships took no more than five days; the *Bristol Star* slowly made it to Savannah in seven days.

After three days, Patrick began to understand their dialect. One of the crew, representing all others, asked why he took this old rusty tub. "To leave England fast," Patrick said. He told them about the girl and thought she cared for him but found it not true.

"There be others," a sailor said. Trying to make him feel better, the sailor said, "After all, there are many ports and many girls, and you will not have a problem finding true love. Remember any port in a storm."

Patrick mixed with the sailors, who adopted him, and he occasionally helped them with simple tasks. Sailors favored him with sea chanties to cheer him up. The chanty *Leaving Liverpool* reminded him of losing Beth, but he never mentioned it to the crew.

Captain Jenkins sat and regaled Patrick with stories about his many years at sea, starting with the clipper ships and then steam-powered ships. He tried to keep Patrick from thinking about Liverpool and losing Beth.

Patrick blamed himself for never declaring his love for her. He had feared she would forsake Colonel Formstone and go with him. Beth Formstone had been his first love, found and lost. Patrick promised from now on that he would speak out and tell of his love if he ever found another. If she rejected him, so be it.

He said his goodbye to the *Bristol Star* crew who wished him smooth sailing and good luck with his love life when he disembarked at Savannah, Georgia, October 29, 1922. He had gained confidence and knowledge of the world that he could never have experienced in the States.

After staying one night at a Savannah boarding house, he bought a passenger train ticket to Chattanooga. From there he caught a train home to Kingsport. Mr. McMasters pick him up at the train station.

"Glad you're home, Patrick," he said. "You look hail and hardy. And still, trim. You may stay with us until you find a place of your own. You didn't eat much Italian food."

"I walked most of it off. Walking and camping is the best way to see Europe except in large cities. I can't believe how mild the weather is now. I thought it would be colder."

"It will be colder before the end of January."

"I still have wanderlust. And, I'll leave for Texas after the first of the year."

As a Christmas presents Lydia McMasters gave Patrick all the European letters he sent them, a journal of his travels, and a traveling secretary. Patrick brought her an expensive pearl necklace and for Mr. McMasters he gave an Italian leather briefcase. The couple tried to make it a merry Christmas for him, but Patrick kept thinking of Beth and what his gift to her would have been. He didn't respond to their efforts. His Christmas wish was to be in Wem. He thought about catching a ship back to England, but maybe the promises made weren't concrete enough. Neither had said "I love you" when they parted Patrick did love her and regretted not telling her in person. The note he wrote her had to substitute. He missed her. Mr. and Mrs. McMasters quietly agreed it was a girl who bothered him, and rightly so.

One morning after Christmas, Lydia, Charles McMasters, and Patrick sat at the kitchen table. "Why are you so down, Patrick? You been home for two months and have not told us anything about your trip. Why so glum?" Charles McMasters asked.

Patrick opened up. "I met a girl on the *Aquitania*. Beth, who is beautiful and fun. We were together all day and most of the night,"

Patrick said and decided not to tell them the whole story. "I left her in Liverpool and toured England and the Continent. When we parted, I didn't tell her of my love, but we agreed to meet after my European journey. She lives near Shrewsbury. When I came back to England, I went to her home to see if she felt the same about me. Long story short, I didn't find her. I regret not having declared my love."

"Why don't you write her? Then, you'll know one way or the other."

"Maybe I will," Patrick couldn't tell about the circumstances that kept him from writing. He had rather keep the beautiful memory of their time together than to know she didn't care for him.

New Year's Eve celebration in Kingsport had been the same as far back as anyone could remember with fireworks and horns at midnight around the countryside. He had no idea where he will be on New Year's Day 1924; Patrick only knew he had to do something to forget Beth Formstone.

Under the administration of Charles McMasters, his trust had grown considerably over the original quarter of a million dollars.

"Do you want to begin drawing money from your fund in addition to your annual five thousand and five hundred dollars?" McMasters asked.

"No, the annual draw has served me well. I'll take two thousand with me and open a checking account at a Kingsport bank. If I need more, I'll draw it. I'm going to visit Uncle Samuel in Texas. I'll want to see the oil fields and perhaps get a job."

"Just as before, write me weekly and tell me where you are. It's easier to transfer money in the States. And, Patrick, I am an only child and cannot have nieces or nephews, I'll feel easier if you call me Uncle Charles."

"I like that, Uncle Charles."

Patrick was at loose ends. He walked around Kingsport. He visited his old school teachers and the friends he left behind to attend Princeton. Patrick didn't know what to do. He decided to go to Texas where he could lose Beth's memory and find satisfaction in a job. Going to Texas was easy; forgetting Beth would be nearly impossible. The letter from Uncle Samuel had said that jobs were plentiful.

The oil companies were hiring policemen without experience, and that would be an excellent place to start.

Patrick had a restless January. On February 18, Lydia and Charles McMasters saw him board the early train to Nashville. He dressed in old clothes and traveled light with just the scarred travelworn valise. He wasn't planning to go to any place where he needed a suit and tie.

CHAPTER 7

BETH AFTER LIVERPOOL

For more than a week, Philip Kelly didn't hear from Beth. Thinking she needed a break from the hassle of dealing with Colonel Formstone's niece and nephew he didn't want to bother her. After the second week, he became concerned and had the constable check her house. The constable reported no one answered the door.

After he received the constable's report, he drove to Beth's cottage to see for himself why she wasn't home. He knocked on her door but heard no movement inside. He rapped harder but heard nothing. Mrs. Peploe, Beth's neighbor, walked up to Kelly.

"Mrs. Formstone is gone. I thought you were together? She came home from Liverpool well over a week ago. and I've not seen her since."

"Something is wrong. Beth has not contacted Mr. Hawkins or me. She could very well be sick. I think I should force the door," Kelly said.

"Please do."

He pushed the door and found it double-locked solid and gave up the idea of forcing the door. "Is there a window that I may open?"

"Yes. A window at the back is large enough for you to crawl through. You may have to break the glass."

Kelly looks inside the window and saw a loose latch.

"Mrs. Pepeloe did you have something that I can slide through the crack and spring the latch?"

"I have a knife."

"Get it please," Kelly said to the retreating Mrs. Peploe."

The old neighbor rushed breathlessly around the house, found the knife, rushed back and handed it to Kelly. He slipped the blade through the crack beneath the seal and jiggled it. The lock moved a bit. He jiggled more. The latch slid back and released the window. Mrs. Peploe watched Kelly pull himself through the window.

"Come to the door," he said, "I'll unlock it."

The two heard nothing inside the dark house.

Mrs. Peploe walked through the kitchen and into the sitting room. "Beth! Beth! Are you here?"

They heard a faint sound from the bedroom in the back of the house.

"She is sick," Mrs. Peploe said and rushed to the bedroom followed by Kelly.

Beth lay across the bed and didn't move when Mrs. Peploe said, "Beth, darling, what has happened to you."

Beth answered with a whisper, "I want to die."

"Beth, I'm here to help," Kelly said. "Tell me what I can do?"

"Philip?"

"Yes, don't talk you'll lose what little strength you have," Mrs. Peploe said. "You have an automobile, Mr. Kelly. She needs to go to the hospital."

"It's parked on the street in front of the house. Help me carry her to the car," Kelly said and picked Beth up. Mrs. Peploe led the way. The old woman got into the back seat of the Crossley and waited for Kelly to lay Beth on her lap. Kelly drove through the streets without caution, all the while blowing his horn. He topped fifty-three miles-per-hour and reached the Royal Shrewsbury Hospital in twenty minutes.

Kelly gathered the limp Beth in his arms which allowed Mrs. Peploe to exit the Crossley and get to the emergency room for help. Two attendants placed Beth on a gurney and wheeled her into a room where a nurse waited. The nurse felt Beth's pulse and looked at her eyes.

"This girl suffers from malnutrition. She's starved," the nurse said.

Doctor Mashburn entered the room and examined Beth.

"She's starved," the nurse said.

"I can see that. Get broth and make this young woman drink as much as she can take without regurgitating. Force her to eat. Who brought her in?"

Standing outside the door, Kelly said, "I did. We found her unconscious in her house."

"Who is she?"

"Beth Formstone."

"Ah, the young wife of Colonel Formstone. I didn't recognize her in this state. Do you know what happened?"

"Mrs. Peploe, her neighbor, can tell you more. Mrs. Peploe?" Kelly called to her.

The old lady sat in a straight-back chair in the family waiting area. She rose and wiped tears from her eyes with a lace handkerchief. "Will she be all right, Mr. Kelly?" she asked.

"Can you tell the doctor about Beth?" Kelly asked.

"How long has it been since she ate? And why hasn't she eaten?" Asked the doctor.

Mrs. Peploe told the doctor, "I last saw her go into her house more than a week ago. She was crying. I thought it was pressure from all the legal goings-on with Colonel Formstone's kin. Then I told her about Patrick McBride, a nice young man who stopped by to see her and the colonel. I think he is Canadian. She began to cry and said she lost someone she loved deeply and didn't know if she would ever see him again. She went into her house. I thought she left with Mr. Kelly the next morning while I was at the market. I believe she went into her house, went to sleep or maybe cried herself to sleep and, grieving for Patrick McBride, didn't get up."

"I've never seen that deep depression before," the doctor said.

"She whispered to me that she wanted to die. God help her. I'll not be saying anymore," Mrs. Peploe said.

"I'm her solicitor," Kelly said. "We'll pay whatever it costs to bring her back to health. I will check on her condition every day."

"I'll stay with her until night and take the train home. I'll be back early tomorrow morning," Mrs. Peploe volunteered.

"Nurse, wake her every two hours and feed her broth. I'll check on her later," Dr. Mashburn said.

CHAPTER 8

MEMPHIS BLUES

Patrick McBride said goodbye to Kingsport when the train moved slowly with jerks caused by cars pulling away and coming back together. It sped up with the whistle screaming warning to clear the tracks far ahead of the train. He settled in a comfortable seat and began reading the first chronicle of the Forsyte Saga. Across the aisle sat a very dapper gentleman beside a middle-aged woman.

"It's the only investment you'll ever have to make," the gentleman said to the woman. "Millions of dollars are being made in Texas by drilling in any spot in West Texas or Oklahoma. I've seen geologist tests that show the land on the Mississippi gulf coast is as productive as any in Texas. You can't miss on a deal like this."

"Before he died, Charles said it was foolish to buy land on speculation, especially oil," she said.

"Charles didn't see this boom coming. If he had, no doubt he would have invested thirty to forty thousand dollars. Poor fellow died before his chance to make a million with the tiny investment of twenty thousand dollars. You don't have to invest but half of that Lucille. Ten thousand dollars will bring in at least two hundred thousand. Almost guaranteed," the dapper man said.

"I don't know, Hubert. I don't feel comfortable investing that much on land I can't see," Lucille said.

"Oh, you make me feel dreadful that you don't trust me," Hubert told her. "Do you think I could ever do something that will hurt my little dumplings? You wrong. I'm looking out for our future."

"If you think it's a wise investment, I'll get the money tomorrow. Why does it have to be in cash?"

"We're buying land secretly. If we write a check, everyone in the bank will know the Northwest Oil Drilling Company is exploring for oil in Mississippi, and land prices will balloon out of control. You understand don't you, Lucille? Keep this investment quiet until I get back from the gulf. You can talk about our investment all you want when the oil gusher comes in. Now kiss me and stop talking about business."

"Hubert Jakes, you're incorrigible. In front of all these people," Lucille said and glanced at Patrick, who had listened to their conversation.

Preparing for the West Texas oil fields, Patrick read about the oil expiration when he returned from Europe. He knew there was no drilling on the gulf coast. The Northwest Oil Drilling Company is a swindle and these people will lose money on a gulf land deal. *Should I warn this couple? It's not my business and maybe he has inside knowledge"*

"Sir, I listened to your conversation and know a little about oil drilling. I think you're stepping into a swindle," Patrick said.

"Didn't your mother ever tell you that it's rude to listen to other people's conversation?" Hubert said.

"Yes. But I must warn you if you're speculating on oil land in Mississippi, you'll waste your money and time," Patrick said.

"The very idea of a stranger, a boy, telling an experienced businessman that he doesn't know of what he is talking. Let's move away from this rude young man, Lucille," Hubert said and helped her from the train seat and moved to another passenger car.

Patrick watched the couple exit the train at Nashville. On the train thoughts of Beth and why he got the wrong impression of her love or interest in him ran through Patrick's mind over and over again. When the train stopped in Nashville, a newsboy came on the train selling morning newspapers.

"I have the *Memphis News-Record*, *Atlanta Constitution*, and *Nashville Banner*. Wednesday, February eighteenth, morning papers, all fresh today. Which one you want, mister?"

"*Memphis News-Record*," Patrick said. He chose that one because Memphis was the last big city before Arkansas.

"That'll be a nickel."

Patrick put a dime and nickel in his hand. The boy looked at the two coins and said, "Hey, thanks, mister."

Patrick went through the violence on the front page and a foreign press article about Benito Mussolini and his private army. The Memphis blues and jazz piqued his interest. He had heard jazz bands in Germany and France, but just a few blues songs. He was behind times in American music and decided to stop in the city and visit a couple of nightclubs. He exited the train at the Memphis Central Station.

He walked to the depot ticket window and asked, "What is the name of a nice hotel away from the train station?"

The clerk sized him up and said, "You can get a cheap room at one of the railroad hotels."

"There's too much noise in one of those. I want quiet."

"The Baumgarten. Suit yourself," was the reply.

Patrick, carrying his beat-up valise, got in the rear seat of a Dodge taxi and told the driver to take him to the Baumgarten Hotel.

"My fare is minimum fifty cents. I'll take you there for seventy-five in advance."

"You think I won't pay?"

"Sorry. I don't think you have any money."

Patrick dug into his pocket, pulled out a dollar and handed it to the driver, "Keep the change."

"Hey, you don't have to do that, mister."

Patrick suddenly realized he looked like a bum. He had not shaved since leaving Kingsport, and his clothes were wrinkled and dirty. Soot from the train had settled on him just like red dust from a country road. "Yeah. I look a mess, but I've been on and off a train for two days," he told the driver.

"I'm sorry mister. You do look like you're down to your last cent. Better pull out your money before you walk up to register at the Baumgarten, or they'll tell you that have no room. And tell them about your travels immediately."

"Thanks for the tip. I'll do that."

Patrick did get the look, but he had two twenty-dollar bills in his hand when he walked up to the registration desk. He signed the register and told the clerk, "I take it you have hot water for a bath."

"Yes, sir."

"I'm accustomed to European accommodations. They seldom have hot water."

"I'm sure you'll find our facilities quite adequate. Our dining room serves dinner until ten o'clock. You have a telephone in your room. If you need anything, call down," the clerk said. "Would you like help with your luggage?"

Patrick lifted his valise up to show the clerk.

"I guess not," the clerk said.

The elevator operator asked what floor.

"Second," Patrick said.

The size of the room and its appointments surprised him. It smelled of elegance and money; there was a small sitting room with table, two comfortable chairs, and a settee. It was the best hotel Patrick had stayed since he left New York two years ago. The bed looked inviting, and he was anxious to try it out that night. The four-poster bed covered with a light blue comforter matched the wallpaper and drapes that hugged the windows of the large bedroom. The bathroom off the bedroom was roomy with a compliment of towels, washcloths, soap, and shampoo.

I could almost swim in this bathtub, he thought. *I may stay for more than a couple of days.*

He shaved and washed off with a damp washcloth. To kill time, he decided to walk around a bit before dinner and see a little of Memphis. He walked out of the hotel but didn't notice the dark clouds off to the west. He strolled down south Main Street. Crossing the street, he turned the corner onto Madison Street and continued to walk. The first raindrops were small, almost like sleet; and wearing a peacoat, he hardly took notice. Then came the deluge of cold rain, normal for February, Patrick learned. Having no umbrella, he found shelter under a store awning.

A lady clerk came to the door and yelled, "You can wait in our store if you'd like."

He did like and stepped into the large clothing store for men and women.

"Thanks. I do appreciate your kindness, miss," he said to the middle-aged clerk. "I hope this storm will subside in a few minutes."

Patrick stood at the closed glass door and watched the street turn into a small river. Fifty yards below the store, street repairs created a dam that kept the water from emptying into the sewer system. The rain came down like someone pouring water from a bucket. A four-door Dodge sedan driven by an old woman stopped in the middle of the street.

"Why is that motorcar stopped?" a clerk asked.

"Drowned out. Dodges tend to do that in heavy rains," Patrick said.

"That woman looks like she is in a panic."

"She is and trying to get out of the car. The water will sweep her away. Let me borrow a raincoat or poncho," Patrick said.

The clerk went to the back of the store and brought back a rubber poncho. "Will this do?"

"Yes," he said and pulled off his peacoat. With poncho in hand, he carefully stepped off the curb onto the flooded street. The water came up almost to his knees and ran swiftly. He struggled to keep on his feet on the way to the stalled Dodge.

Standing on the running board, the lady greeted him with, "Young man, please get me out of here."

He wrapped the poncho around her and picked her up. It was slow going back to the store with the swirling water and driving rain. He sat the old lady down inside the store, where a small crowd gathered and applauded.

The two were shivering like leaves in a strong wind when they entered the store.

"Well, I'm wet, but, young man, you look like a drowned cat. You'd better dry out, or you'll catch a cold," the old lady said. "Thank you so much. I must say that I was terrified. What is your name?"

"Patrick McBride, ma'am. And you are welcome."

A man tapped him on the shoulder. "Come with me. We'll get you dried out," the man said and led Patrick to a dressing room in the back of the store.

"I'm Jonathan Jacobs." He handed Patrick a towel and blanket. "Wrap up in this blanket and get warm. I'll bring some clothes for you," Jacobs said.

Jacob's Department Store. I guess he is the owner, Patrick mused. He pulled off his beat-up hiking clothes that were wet inside and out and shucked his wet clothes. Patrick shivered while drying off.

Minutes later Jacobs knocked on the dressing room door and looked at Patrick wrapped in a warm blanket. "I believe this may fit you. I have underwear coming," he said and handed Patrick a pair of pants, a shirt, shoes and socks. The shoes were a size too big, but Patrick didn't complain.

Jacobs soon knocked on the door and handed him a pair of shorts. After dressing, Patrick felt much better and walked up to the front of the store.

"You are the man of the hour," an attractive young lady said. "Do you know who you saved?"

"No, ma'am."

"She's Judge Webster's wife."

"Since I'm not from Memphis. Who is Judge Webster?" Patrick asked.

"Superior court judge and a good friend of Boss Crump. When you're ready, it will be my pleasure to show you Memphis. I'm Laura Hemphill."

The rescued woman came from the lady's dressing room in a new dress.

"It is Patrick, is it not?" Judge Webster's wife asked.

"Yes, ma'am. Patrick McBride."

"Tell me about yourself, Patrick."

"Not much to tell. I have been traveling for a year. Mostly in Europe. I'm on my way to the West Texas oil fields and stopped in Memphis to rest a couple of days."

"What kind of work did you do in Europe?"

"I didn't work. I have no family. My dad died and left some money. I decided to see some of Europe before settling down. I not sure what I want to do," Patrick said.

"I didn't introduce myself. I'm Emma Webster. Oh, here comes a Memphis policeman. I guess I'm in trouble for leaving my car on the street."

The uniformed policeman shook the rain off his hat and raincoat before he came into the store. Patrick met him at the door.

"Officer, this lady's car engine drowned out, and she needs help to get it out of the street. I'm sure we can have it towed when it stops raining," Patrick said.

Ignoring Patrick, the policeman said, "Mrs. Webster, I've taken care of your car. It will be in Sander's Garage. I have someone coming to see you home."

"Thank you, Lester. Will you find a ride for this young man? He took me out of the car in all this terrible weather. Where do you want to go, Patrick?"

"I'm at the Baumgarten."

"I'll send a car for him, Mrs. Webster."

"My clothes should be dry by now. I'll go back and change," Patrick said.

"No need for that. The clothes you have on are yours," Jacobs said. "I'll have the others cleaned and sent to your hotel. And here is your peacoat."

The rain had calmed down to a steady drizzle by the time a police car came for Mrs. Webster. She hugged Patrick goodbye with a promise to remember him. Patrick's ride came in a vehicle driven by a uniformed policeman.

"You must be special for this service," the policeman said. "I guess you're either kin to the judge or the missus."

"Does it rain like this in Memphis all the time?"

"No, it snows," the policeman answered.

"Good afternoon, Mr. McBride," the clerk said when Patrick passed by the registration desk.

"Nice shirt, Mr. McBride," the elevator operator said and took him to the second floor without asking what floor he wanted.

Patrick was tired. He had not gotten the afternoon nap he promised himself and since he was not hungry, decided to take a hot bath and go to sleep. Patrick soaked in warm water for forty minutes and almost fell asleep. After drying off with a large bath towel, he put on underwear and lay in the bed to rest before going to dinner. He slept and dreamed that he held Beth in his arms. Her hair smelled clean and soft. She pulled back and smiled her enchantment. The telephone rang harshly.

CHAPTER 9

Philip Kelly Helps Beth

It was Philip Kelly that brought Beth out of her depression. He stayed and talked with her every minute he could spare. He brought her flowers and made her laugh at his not-so-funny jokes. She began eating after a week and asked Doctor Mashburn if he would dismiss her from hospital. He said yes.

Kelly drove Beth home where Mrs. Peploe waited. The effects of her depression left her weak and Kelly carried her into the house and put her in bed. "I don't want to leave you," Kelly told Beth. "But I have business to attend to."

"You've done enough, and I thank you," she said.

"You're in good hands with Mrs. Peploe," Kelly said and kissed her forehead. "I will come by after work,

After Kelly left, Mrs. Peploe said, "He's a nice young man, and you'll not find anyone better. He is quite fond of you."

Beth thought *I wish it were that simple. I can't get Patrick out of my mind, and I don't want to.*

Mrs. Peploe and neighbors made Christmas cheery for Beth with a Christmas party. Kelly brought her presents of perfume and a scarf. Kelly and Beth talked long after the Christmas party.

"You never told me how you met McBride, the man you love, who abandoned you," Kelly said sarcastically.

Beth began, "On the way back to Liverpool from New York, I met this boy, man, and I fell for him. He set out to tour the Continent for a year and promised to meet me on a certain day the next year. A hundred times I wanted to go with him, but he understood the .

situation with Gaddy and would never let me. We never talked about love or marriage; it was a given. He didn't tell me he loved me nor I to him. That certain day came in October and found me with you in Birmingham trying to sort out Gaddy's will," Beth said.

"We accomplished absolutely nothing, as I recall."

"You convinced me to stay that Saturday night and catch the early train to Liverpool. Patrick and I were to meet at the Britannia Adelphi on October 22nd. I inquired at the hotel desk, and he had gone that morning back to the States. I tried to find what ship he booked, but no ships, except three freighters, had left Liverpool. I found his note when I returned home from Liverpool. He wrote that he loved me and regretted not telling me. He thought you and I had something going on and wished me happiness. He left no address or where I can contact him."

"You do have a dilemma. Whatever gave Patrick the impression of you and me?"

"Mrs. Peploe told him she thought there was something more than a working relationship. She thought so since we spend so much time together."

"I'm sorry to hear this. You can give all the inheritance to the Bandon children, and it will be over. You'll be free to pursue this unfaithful character." Kelly told her.

"No. Gaddy trusted me to distribute his money the way he wanted, and I will not betray that trust. I firmly believe that Patrick McBride will concur."

"What difference does it make? You'll never see Patrick McBride again. Believe me, I know Irishmen, and he found another as soon as he got to America," Kelly said.

"I don't believe that for a minute. It sounds like you're jealous of Patrick."

"As a friend, I am concerned what happens in your life and don't want to see you depressed again, ever."

"I won't be depressed by keeping Patrick McBride in my thoughts and remembering his face and touch that's why I will search until I find him."

Yeah. Philip thought. *You are a lovesick fool. He'll never come back to England, and you'll never see him again.*

CHAPTER 10

A JOB FOR MCBRIDE

The phone startled him awake. He could see daylight coming through a small open crease in the drapes. When he went into the sitting room to answer the phone, he thought, *Still daylight. I'll have plenty of time to dress and go to the dining room.*

"Hello," he answered.

"Is this Mr. Patrick McBride?"

"Yes."

"Mr. McBride, my name is Sandra, and I'm calling for Judge Webster. He would like for you to have lunch with him at the Factors Club."

"Tomorrow?"

"No, today. If it's convenient."

"Wait one minute please."

He put the receiver down and walked to the window pulled the drapes back and the morning sun blinded him for a few seconds. To clear his mind, he moved slowly back to the telephone.

"I'll have lunch with Judge Webster today. What time and where is the Factors Club?"

"At twelve-thirty. The club is at Front and Union Streets. It's within walking distance from your hotel. The staff will give you directions. I'll tell the Judge. I'm sure he will be delighted you accepted his invitation. Thank you, Mr. McBride. Goodbye."

"Goodbye,"

Patrick picked up his pocket watch from the table and checked the time. *Damn. It's nine o'clock. I can't believe I slept that long. I'll go down for a coffee and toast. I want to be hungry at lunch.*

After breakfast, he walked to Jacobs Department Store. Mr. Jacobs appeared when Patrick entered the store.

"Morning, Mr. Jacobs."

"Good morning, Mr. McBride. Did you come for your clothes?"

"Yes and no. I have an invitation to lunch at the Factors Club, whatever that is, and I want to dress appropriately. I know you can tell me what I should buy."

The store owner chose a dress shirt, tie, suit, overcoat and gray hat. "It's appropriate, but a little pricey at thirty dollars. You can pay for it on time," Jacobs said, "We can have it ready for you in an hour."

"No. I pay cash."

He handed Jacobs a twenty and ten. The store owner shook his head when he left.

Patrick soon found out the Factors Club membership came from old money as well as old families of Memphis. He entered the club and saw a desk manned by a well-dressed clerk who looked askance at him.

"May I help you, sir?"

"Judge Webster invited me to lunch here."

"And your name sir?"

"Patrick McBride."

The clerk pulled a pad from his desk drawer and went down a list of names with his finger. "Yes. Patrick McBride. Lunch with Judge Webster." He picked up a small bell and rang it softly.

Almost immediately a maître d' came from a door on the side of the large lobby and motioned Patrick to follow him to a lounge. There were comfortable chairs along with a leather couch strategically placed around a fireplace. Several writing tables were lined up along the mahogany panel wall.

"Judge Webster awaits you in the dining room," the maître d' said and walked toward another door on the side of the lounge. Patrick followed.

The judge rose to greet him as he entered the dining room.

"You're Patrick McBride?"

"Yes, sir."

"I'm Judge Otis Webster. I'm glad to meet you. Emma is extremely grateful to you for having pulled her out of the car. She is scared to death of water and thought if she stayed in the car, it would fill with water and drown her. I also appreciate your saving her,"

"She was perfectly safe in the car, but I saw her getting out. The swift water would have knocked her down. That could have meant disaster."

"Emma says you are a hero and wants to reward you but thinks it is bad form to give you money."

"I didn't take her out of the water for a reward. It will be bad form to take an award."

"I understand you've been bumming around for a while," the judge said. "Ever think about settling down?"

"I have, but I've not found anything I want to do or any place to do it in," Patrick said.

After ordering asparagus soup with sweet ice tea for two, the judge said, "Asparagus soup is the chef's special dish. You'll enjoy it. Now, tell me a little about yourself."

"Born and grew up in Kingsport, Tennessee in the area where my family lived for well over a hundred years. I studied at Princeton University, and my dad died before I entered my senior year. My mother died three years before. I have an uncle that I've seen five times in my life. My dad's law partner is closer than any relative. That said, Uncle Samuel invited me to visit him in West Texas to get better acquainted. I'm on my way there."

"Your father was a lawyer? Are you the son of Shumate McBride?"

"Yes."

"I knew him well. We passed the bar together. He was a good man and lawyer."

Patrick nodded, "I agree. And a good father."

"Why did you quit Princeton?"

"It was dad's idea for me to go there. It was his alma mater. I didn't like Princeton."

"Didn't want to study law?"

"No, sir. I guess my dad's death hit me harder than I thought. I haven't found what to do with my life."

"How you fixed for money?"

"I have a trust that furnishes me an annual amount of money. If I need more, I'll supplement it when I get a job. I'm not married and don't need much to live on."

"You've been exposed to law, while you're waiting to discover what you want to do, join our police. The department is recruiting candidates now. How does that sound?"

"I can use a job."

"Good enough. I'll call the police commissioner and tell him of your interest. He'll tell Chief Roscoe Flynn you're coming down. You shouldn't have a problem hiring on. In fact, after we finish lunch, we'll drive down to city hall. The police station is in that building."

"Thank you, sir," Patrick said and thought of the company police job in Texas.

After using a club phone, Judge Webster motioned to Patrick to follow him. On the way to Memphis police station, the judge kept up chatter about Memphis and what a great place it was to settle. And how modern it was. The people passing on the street said hello to the judge or tipped their hats. Patrick took these courteous actions as signs of respect and admiration.

Judge Webster and Patrick entered the police station. The judge startled the desk sergeant. He dropped his work and almost stood at attention.

"Judge Webster, sir. How can I help you?"

"Is Chief Flynn here?"

"Yes. I'll show you to the chief's office," the desk sergeant said.

"I know where it is," he said. "Come with me, Patrick."

They walked to the back of the police station to the chief's office. A secretary sat outside his office door.

"Good afternoon, Judge Webster," she said. "Go in. The chief is waiting for you."

Chief Flynn rose from his desk when they entered the office.

"Judge Webster," he said and looked at Patrick. "What do we owe this visit to."

"You've been recruiting policemen. This young man wants to join, and on my recommendation, he'll be an asset to your force.

Chief Flynn meet Patrick McBride."

Flynn offered his hand across the desk to Patrick, who said, "Good to meet you, sir."

"Likewise," said the chief.

"You will expedite his application and test, chief?"

"You bet."

"I'll check with you later, Patrick," The judge said as he left the office.

Chief looked out the door and made sure Judge Webster was out of hearing distance, "I don't like nobody telling me who to and who not to hire. I don't care if he is Crump's judge." Flynn motioned Patrick to follow him.

Patrick held back and said nothing, knowing that it was the best possible course in this situation. At his office door, he said to his secretary, "Mrs. George, take this Irish boy to personnel and have him fill out an application and tell Chambers I want to see him."

There were curious stares at Patrick when he and Mrs. George walked to personnel.

"Chief says for you to have this fellow fill out an application to join the force, and to go see him now."

Lieutenant Chambers took an application from a bin where forms were kept and handed it to Patrick.

"Fill this out and bring it back to me." Chambers said and pointed to a desk with several pencils. In a few minutes, Patrick handed the completed application to the personnel officer who looked at it and then to the applicant.

"So, you've got three years of college, but no experience in police work. You one of them smart boys the judge is always talking about?"

"I don't know the judge that well."

"He knows you well enough. You got the job without taking a test."

"I'll be glad to take the test."

"Chief Flynn says no need for a test, so you don't take no test. Tomorrow morning be here by seven o'clock. Deputy Chief Sergeant Flaherty will assign you a beat, and he'll issue a number and badge. He'll take care of a chit to draw money from the pay clerk for a uniform. Ask Flaherty where to buy the uniform. You'll draw what you need as a patrolman from the equipment room. The sergeant at the arsenal will issue you a pistol and ammunition. I hope you know how to handle a handgun. Do you?"

"Yes, sir. I do."

"We'll see about that on the practice range."

That night, Patrick wrote home:

February 1923

Dear Folks,

You will not believe that within two days of landing in Memphis I have a job. The Memphis Police Department hired me at the behest of Judge Otis Webster. He knew dad, and you may know him, Uncle Charles. I'll tell you the whole story when I come home at Easter.

Yours,

CHAPTER 11

LAURA HEMPHILL

When Patrick McBride carried Emma Webster into Jacobs Department Store, he shivered like a leaf in a windstorm. Laura Hemphill fell in love with him then and there. She wanted to hold him until he stopped shaking, but regrettably, couldn't. Before he left the store, Laura spoke to him about Judge Webster and offered to show him around Memphis. Patrick walked out before she found out how she could contact him but just knew she would find him.

That night she couldn't sleep for thinking of him. *How silly of me,* she thought. He may be married or engaged. He could be a horrible person, but she knew better. She could tell by his face. She heard him say that he was on the way to the Texas oil fields. Impossible. She couldn't believe it. Before she saw Patrick McBride, she didn't believe in love at first sight.

Laura began asking questions about Patrick, and no one knew him or anything about him. She checked every hotel until she came to the Baumgarten.

"Do you have a Patrick McBride registered there?"

"We don't give out that information miss, unless you're a relative."

"I'm Laura, Patrick's sister."

"Yes. Mr. McBride was registered here but has checked out."

Laura's heart dropped.

"He moved to the Almadura apartments on Stonewall."

"Thank you. I wanted to surprise Patrick, and now I can."

He's still in Memphis and looking for a job, unless he had found one already. She began to ask customers who came into Jacobs

Department Store. Mrs. Gloria Flaherty gave her the answer she wanted.

"Patrick McBride is that new man working for my husband. He says he'll make a good policeman."

"Does he work at the station?"

"No. Patrick has a beat. I don't know where."

After Mrs. Flaherty left, Laura telephoned the police station.

"Memphis police," the duty sergeant answered.

"Sergeant Flaherty, please."

It took a few seconds, but it seemed like forever to Laura.

"Sergeant Flaherty speaking."

"Sergeant, this is Laura Hemphill. Your wife said that you have a Patrick McBride working there."

"Yes, we do but not at the station. He patrols Court Avenue and 2nd Street."

"I know where that is."

"If you have a complaint, miss, I can help with that."

"He is an acquaintance. No complaint."

"McBride's shift ends at four o'clock," the sergeant said and thought that he shouldn't have told her. He had never made that mistake before. She could be a deserted wife. He shrugged it off.

"Thanks, Sergeant Flaherty," she hung up the telephone and found Mr. Jacobs. "I have an important thing I have to do this afternoon; may I leave at three?"

"So, meeting a boy? Then, take off at three."

It took Laura almost twenty minutes to walk to 2nd Street. She and saw a uniformed policeman turn down Court Avenue. It was Patrick McBride strolling down the street. She hurried and caught up with him.

He was thinking of Beth when Laura said, "Is that you, Mr. McBride?"

"Ma'am?"

"You don't remember me, do you? I'm Laura Hemphill. I work at Jacobs Department Store. I saw you bring Judge Webster's wife out of her car in that flood."

"I do remember you. How could I ever forget?" He lied.

After Beth, he didn't notice girls as much as before. He had forgotten Laura Hemphill, but he didn't know why. Her emerald green eyes took his breath away. The rest of her—creamy skin, dark hair and shapely body—almost stopped his heart. He compared her to Beth, but it didn't work; they were different.

"That day? Or me?"

"I guess a little of both," said Patrick.

"Look at you, Patrick, all handsome in uniform. It is Patrick, isn't it? I heard you became a policeman and thought I would eventually run into you."

"You have a good memory," Patrick thought about shift change in fifteen minutes. "I'm glad you ran into me."

"If I'm not too forward for a southern lady, I'd like to have a coffee or tea and hear about your police work," Laura said.

"When?" He needed to talk to someone, preferably a young woman.

"Anytime."

"I get off in ten minutes," Patrick said, checking his pocket watch.

"Should I wait here?"

"I'll have to check out at headquarters and change into civvies. You'll have a long wait."

"How about if I walk with you to the police station and wait there?"

"That's a good idea. Walk with me down Court Avenue. My relief will meet me at the Court call box."

Laura hung back when Patrick met Albert Sidney Smith at the call box on Court. Smith looked askance at Patrick, who took her hand and gently pulled her beside him.

"Laura meet Albert Sidney Smith, a fine officer and a credit to the Memphis police force. Albert Sidney meet Laura Hemphill, the prettiest girl in Memphis."

Albert Sidney did a half bow and said, "You, my friend, are half right. Julie, my girl, is prettier. Although I'll admit, Miss Hemphill comes in a very close second."

"It's not nice to talk about a lady in her presence. But you may continue, and I'll close my ears," Laura said.

"This is getting too deep, and I've got a beat to walk. Nice meeting you, Laura. Maybe we can go on a double date when we're not on duty. You are officially relieved, McBride.”

“And I will depart from you,” Patrick said, “knowing that Memphis and its environs will be safe until relieved by another worthy guard in blue.”

“Ah, get the hell out of here and take this beautiful lady out to eat,” Albert Sidney said.

Laura and Patrick slowly walked toward the Adams Street police headquarters.

“Do you two always talk that way?” Asks Laura.

“Yes and no. Today, it was to impress you with our levity.”

“I don’t believe it. Why should Albert Sidney want to impress me?”

“He thought he could help me out with you. He always tries to fix me up with a girl. Most have a great personality but in person . . .” He left that unsaid.

“Do you think I’m pretty?”

He looked at her again and saw that she was indeed pretty. Never had he seen emerald green eyes with a flicker of fire. He felt lucky to have her with him to make Albert Sidney Smith envious.

“Laura Hemphill you’re not pretty . . . you are beautiful,” Patrick said.

Laura grabbed his hand and pulled it to her cheek. “You didn’t need to say that, but it means a lot coming from you.”

After I change into civilian clothes, we’ll go to the Baumgarten for coffee.”

Over coffee and tea cakes they learned about each other, and both liked what they heard.

“My mother insisted on Myra Sharpe College and Finishing School for Young Ladies. I finished two years ago. I have a teacher’s certificate, but I don’t want to teach school. Mr. Jacobs, a family friend, offered me a job in his clothing store. He said he would teach me merchandising, and he’s lived up to his promise. Merchandising is not for me, though. I stay there because I feel an obligation to Mr. Jacobs. I won’t leave Memphis. It’s a good place to be now. It’s coming out of past doldrums and on the move. I see business booming. The Mississippi River is still a major transportation system for freight. Although I haven't found what I want to do for the rest of my life, I believe I'll find it here. I plant my feet in concrete right here," Laura finished her story.

"You didn't mention your father."

"He died in the war and is buried in France. I don't remember much about him; he made the army a career. He was gone for most of my formative years."

Patrick said. "That's much the same as my experience, except I didn't finish Princeton."

He paused for reflection and continued, "When dad died, I just lost all interest in higher education. I bummed around Europe for a year taking odd jobs here and there before I got homesick. Europe didn't solve my problem; I still don't know what to do with my life. Uncle Samuel invited me to come out to West Texas and work in the oil fields. Although the McMasters are closer than my uncle, they are not blood. I want to get to know my uncle, so I'm on my way to Texas." Patrick paused and thought about his situation.

"I will stay with the Memphis Police Department for a year to give the Judge and Emma Webster their chance to convince me to stay in Memphis. That's a tall order; I don't think anyone or anything can keep me from Texas."

He thought about Emma Webster's invitation to Sunday supper and thought it would be nice to bring a young lady with him. "Laura, this may be too soon. Mrs. Webster and the Judge invited me to Sunday supper this week, would you like to go with me? I need a female to see if Mrs. Webster has something up her sleeve that involves me."

"That sounds intriguing. If you can wrangle an invitation for me, I'll be your spy."

CHAPTER 12

DINNER WITH THE WEBSTERS

Patrick called Mrs. Webster the next day. She was delighted to have female company instead of having to listen to men talk baseball and fishing. The rest of the week he thought about the girl he had briefly seen the day of the rescue. Looking back, she was that pretty girl. He was a little suspicious about meeting her on his rounds. But Patrick dismissed his suspicions as being a policeman.

Patrick asked Laura up to his apartment to wait for the judge's driver. She rang the bell at four o'clock, and he answered. "Come in. We won't have to wait long."

Laura looked around and said, "How can you afford such luxury?"

"I got a deal being the first renter. I agreed to be a spokesman. For that, the owners reduced the rent and furnished a household cleaning service. They may show the apartment any time I'm away." He didn't like to lie about his wealth, but he thought it better not to let people know.

"Would you like something to drink while we wait? Ice tea? Coffee?"

"No thanks. Are you trying to get me drunk and take advantage of me?"

He didn't know how to answer her.

"I made you blush. Can I get drunk on tea or coffee? I don't think so."

"You have a perverted sense of humor."

The doorbell rang.

"That's the driver," he said and was relieved their conversation ended.

It took five minutes to reach Judge Webster's house. The driver held the door open for the couple to exit the car. Patrick and Laura walked up a paved path between blooming azaleas and early spring flowers.

"I feel rich," Laura said.

"Don't get used to it. The dream will end in a couple of hours."

Patrick, expecting a butler, was surprised when Judge Webster answered the door.

"Come into my humble home," the judge said. "We'll leave your coats and hat on the rack."

Anything but humble, Laura thought and took Patrick's arm.

"Emma said we will have ice tea in the living room," the judge told them.

He pointed out each room on each side of a long hall.

"This is my study. That's Emma's sewing room. Keeps us separated. Prevents arguments. I don't like to lose, after all, I am a lawyer and a judge," he said with a serious tone.

Emma Webster met them at the living room door. "Oh, Patrick, I'm so glad you could come. And you, young lady—you're lucky to have your fellow."

"Mrs. Webster, this is Laura Hemphill."

"I agree wholeheartedly. I *am* fortunate," Laura said and took Patrick's hand.

He noticed how Laura never missed a chance to hold his hand. It felt right, and maybe her pretense would keep at a distance, the girls looking to hook him into marriage. He didn't want to get involved with anyone in Memphis.

Judge Webster promised Emma he would not talk business. He violated that trust when he took Patrick into his private office.

"May I get you something a little stronger than coffee, Patrick?"

"No, sir. I will occasionally drink beer. But no hard liquor."

"Good boy. How is the police job working out?"

"I like the job. The merchants on my beat are nice, and I try to be helpful. The hours aren't bad, and I get plenty of exercise. Overall, it's great for me."

"How about your fellow officers?"

Patrick hesitated. "Sergeant Flaherty has been helpful, and I made friends with Albert Sidney Smith. He patrols second shift."

"And others?"

He paused again but decided to tell it like it is. "It's been cold at roll call. They resent how I got the job. I can hear them whispering behind my back. I go by the book and hope to get a perfect score on sixth-month evaluation. I don't intend to give up. I'll be there until hell freezes over."

"I'm sorry to hear that. Maybe I can find something more to your liking."

"Thanks for your concern. But I want to stay where I am," Patrick said.

"Very well."

To Emma's surprise and delight, Laura helped serve and do dishes afterward. Then, the four talked until way past dark. Patrick finally said he had to get her back to her apartment.

"Does your apartment have a curfew?" Emma asked.

"No, ma'am. Patrick is such a stickler for time. You're a wonderful hostess. I hate to leave, but the carriage will turn into a pumpkin soon."

Emma winked at Laura, who winked back.

Their host and hostess said goodbye at the door.

"Thanks for your wonderful Sunday supper, Mrs. Webster. You're a great cook," Patrick said.

"I echo that," Laura said as she took Patrick by the hand.

"You two are welcome anytime," Judge Webster said. "Patrick, remember what I told you."

"Yes, sir. I will."

"Laura, remember what I told you," Emma said.

"You bet I will."

The two began their walk to the waiting car, leaving their host standing in the door. They overheard Emma tell the judge, "They make such a lovely couple, don't they, Otis?"

"Emma, you always get in trouble playing Cupid," he told her.

Laura opened her apartment door and stood there while Patrick thanked her for coming and said what a good time he had.

"Thank you. Emma is great. Too bad they never had children. But they are very fond of you. She told me they feel as though you were sent to be the son they never had."

"Ah, come on, that's not a good joke."

March 1923
Dear Folks,

Laura Hemphill and I had dinner with Judge Webster and Emma, his wife. I met Laura Hemphill the day when I carried Emma Webster into a clothing store during a rainstorm. Although quite rich, the Websters are friendly, down-to-earth people.

Yours,

CHAPTER 13

THE OFFER TO THE BANDONS

The train to Birmingham ran through the most beautiful part of England. With the cool nights and gentle rain, the month of May brought out the bright green plants and trees. *I don't think I could live any other place on Earth*, Beth thought.

Philip Kelly, going through legal papers, sat beside Beth unaware of the countryside. He looked up from his work and smiled at Beth. "I hope the Bandons' lawyer isn't meeting us to push for an outrageous settlement," he said.

That afternoon, Ralph Hawkins, Philip Kelly and William Grant, the siblings' lawyer, sat at a table in the conference room furnished by the registry.

"If they are not here in ten minutes, we're leaving," Hawkins told Grant.

"I'm sure they will be along shortly. Let's be patient," Grant replied.

The two rushed into the room with two minutes to spare.

"Grant, you better not have started without us or, you're fired. I don't see that whore, so you're smart not to include her," Banny said.

Grant gave Banny an unfriendly smile, "We couldn't start without the one who thinks he is most important."

"Stop wasting time. Let's get started," Beatrice said.

"Okay. What do you want?" Hawkins asked.

"All or nothing," they replied in unison.

"Let me do the negotiating," Grant told them.

Banny Bandon said, "We'll see that that slut gets nothing."

"Poor Uncle Gadsden. He caught him in her web, like a spider. She doesn't deserve anything," Beatrice said.

"We refuse to consider 'all or nothing' and unless we have a starting point. I think we'll accomplish nothing in this meeting. Mrs. Formstone is willing to give something reasonable," Hawkins said.

"Beth 'Whoever' can't offer something she doesn't have. The inheritance is not hers to give. She seduced Uncle Gadsden. He was weak when it came to women. She'll get nothing."

William Grant blanched, "We'll meet at a later date, Mr. Hawkins. Name the day and time. It's better if just the two of us meet."

"Very good," Hawkins said.

Ralph Hawkins and Philip Kelly left the room and heard Banny shout, "You'll not meet anyone without our being present, you hear me, Grant."

"If it were me, the Bandon siblings would be without a solicitor now," Philip said.

Philip Kelly sat across the table from Beth and told her what had happened at the meeting. "We were prepared to offer them a hundred thousand pounds each, but the rapscallion Banny wouldn't consider any offer. His sister backs him up. They want all or nothing."

Beth wilted before Philip's eyes, and he took her hand. It was a gesture of sympathy Beth appreciated, but Philip had other ideas. He hadn't said anything to her about a proposal of marriage, but now her will was weak and the perfect time to pop the question. Philip Kelly needed Beth and felt she need him more than ever as a lawyer and husband.

The next Sunday afternoon, Philip said, "We are good together, are we not, Beth?"

"Yes, we are."

"I love you, Beth, and I want you to be my wife. Will you?"

Before she accepted, she thought about Patrick and how much she loved him. If she found him, would she and he feel the same? And if she married Philip, and Patrick came back what would she do? Patrick and Beth were together a week, a very short time to fall in love, but Beth couldn't deny he became a large part of her life that she could not give up. Deep down in her heart, she knew nothing would ever take his place, and they belonged together.

She admitted love for Philip, but it was more a quiet friend type of love and nothing passionate. She enjoyed being with Philip. He was kind and gentle, and she would have a wonderful life with him. If she searched and never found Patrick, she knew Philip wouldn't wait, and the opportunity for happiness with Philip would be over. But her love for Patrick overrode the sensible solution.

"I'm so sorry, Philip. I cannot accept your proposal now. I hold out a hope that Patrick McBride comes to find me. I may have time to search for him in America after we sort out this situation with Gaddy's will."

"Just remember, I will not wait forever," Philip Kelly replied.

"Oh, if I only knew that Patrick McBride had forgotten me."

Beth Formstone dreamed of Patrick many nights and almost the same dream. She saw him kissing the bride, and it wasn't her. For some reason she didn't understand, she began to dream of Patrick and herself. He held her in his arms and told her never to leave him. She wanted to go to a dream interpreter but dismissed the idea for fear it might mean something she shouldn't know or didn't want to know.

After Philip kissed her that Sunday evening, he didn't try again, and Beth didn't encourage any further action.

CHAPTER 14

RIGHTEOUS KILL

Patrick leisurely walked his beat and stopped to talk to Mr. Lane, owner of Lane's Fine Jewelry Store. He heard them before he saw what was happening. Two men ran out of Piggly-Wiggly two doors down.

First one shouted, "Stay in there, and no one will get hurt."

The other pointed a gun at the storefront and fired.

"You stupid shit. I told you not to shoot," the first one shouted.

"That old bastard was pulling a gun from under the counter," the second one screamed.

Patrick pulled his Colt .45 from his holster and shouted, "Police! Drop the gun. Stand where you are."

The two robbers looked at him walking toward them holding his gun pointed upward. The first one said, "Shoot the cop."

The second robber pointed his gun at Patrick but didn't have time to pull the trigger before Patrick dropped to one knee and fired. The robber went down with a bullet in his heart, and after a couple of twitches, he lay still.

The one with the money bag put up his hands. "I don't have no gun. Don't shoot. Don't shoot," he said and dropped the bag.

Patrick handcuffed the robber to a metal hitching post left over from horse-drawn buggy days, picked up the bag of money, and asked no one in particular, "Anybody hurt inside?"

"Fellow's been shot in the shoulder. I got an ambulance coming," a store clerk said.

The man Patrick shot lay on the street in a puddle of blood.

Patrick bent down and felt for a pulse. There was none. A grocery clerk, wearing a white apron, stood watching.

"I need your apron," he told the clerk.

The clerk untied the apron and handed it to Patrick who covered the robber's face and chest with it. Patrick gave the money bag to the grocery clerk, "Take care of this."

People, like termites, came out of nearby stores and gathered in front of the Piggly-Wiggly to see what had happened.

"I saw it all," a bystander said, "He shot one of 'em when they come out of the store."

"No, he didn't, he shouted for them to drop the gun, then he shot the one with the gun."

"Yeah, these two came out of Piggly-Wiggly. One had a gun and shot a customer for no reason."

"That's the cop that shot that robber in the chest from way back there. That's a hell of a shot."

"Stand back. This lady fainted."

Patrolman Tommy Blalock came up to Patrick and said, "I called it in. Lieutenant Byers is on the way."

"I'm glad to see you here. I can't control these people."

Both patrolmen began moving people from around the robber's body to make room for the ambulance attendants to pick up the wounded grocery customer. The live robber handcuffed to the hitching post kept quiet.

"Clear the way. Clear the way," Lieutenant Billy Byers, chief of foot patrol, bellowed in a bass voice and cleared a way where the two patrolmen stood. "What the hell is going on here? McBride, did you shoot someone? You discharged your weapon on a city street. I'll hang your ass out."

"Who's that cop?" someone asked.

"That's Old Lieutenant Byers. He thinks he's God's gift to Memphis," a bystander said.

"Okay, Blalock, what happened here?"

"When I got here there was a crowd around a dead man laying over there and a wounded civilian in the store. McBride had handcuffed that man to the hitching post. We have been trying to keep these people back. That's all I know."

The lieutenant turned to Patrick and said, "Okay, smart guy, explain yourself, and it better be good."

"The man handcuffed to the rail over there and the man covered by the apron were robbing Piggly-Wiggly," Patrick said. "I saw what was happening when they came out of the store. One with the gun fired into the store. I yelled for them to stop. The one with the gun pointed it at me. I dropped to my knee and shot him before he fired. That's about it."

"Are there witnesses?"

"Sure. Store clerks and bystanders."

"Where were you when you discharged your weapon?" Byers asked.

"In front of that store," Patrick indicated with his thumb the store two doors down.

"You fired from there?"

"Pretty close. I walked toward the two robbers."

"Give me your gun and badge, you turd. I'm putting you on report. No judge is gonna get you off."

"How about a district attorney, Lieutenant Byres? You think a DA is going to indict if he's the principal witness?"

"Who the hell are you?"

"District Attorney Robert Ingraham at your service, Lieutenant Byres."

"Oh, sorry for the language, sir. I didn't recognize you. You saw it all?"

"I did. This patrolman went strictly by the book. He walked, with his pistol pointing into the air, directly toward the robbers, shouting for them to stand down, and glanced to make sure there was no one behind them. The shooter pointed his gun. Patrolman, what is your name?"

"McBride, sir, Patrick McBride."

"Patrolman McBride shouted for the two men to drop the gun and stand still. They turned and looked at him walking toward them. One told the gunman to shoot the cop. The gunman pointed his pistol at McBride, who took one knee and shot him. The other one shouted he had no gun and gave up. McBride handcuffed him, assessed the situation and began checking for injured bystanders. I think he was quite cool under fire, and he is a credit to the Memphis Police Department.”

“Thank you, sir. Would you mind giving a statement? Just routine, you know,” Byers asked.

“Not at all. I have nothing to do. I’ll go to police headquarters now. I believe you should give Patrolman McBride back his badge, Byers.”

“Oh, I will, sir. Patrick, here’s your badge. I’ll have to keep your piece for a couple of hours.”

“Thanks, Lieutenant Byers,” Patrick said.

Byers, followed by Patrick and District Attorney Ingraham walked to police headquarters.

“What happened?” Desk Sargeant Michaels asked.

“Robbery at the Piggly-Wiggly on Second Street. One down, Blalock is taking the other to lockup.”

“Who shot the one down?”

“McBride.”

“McBride? Is that why you took his gun? He’s still wearing his badge.”

“Looked like a righteous kill. Take care of this for me,” the lieutenant handed the pistol to the desk sergeant, who watched Byers followed by McBride and the civilian, head back to chief’s office

By that time, headquarters was buzzing about the foiled robbery. Police officers sniggered and pointed at McBride as the three passed. They looked at each other and grinned knowing what was about to happen to their fellow officer. Flynn waited at his office door for them to arrive.

“I see you finally got that snot, McBride,” Flynn said to Byers.

“McBride killed one of the men robbing Piggly-Wiggly. The other is in custody.”

“I know that. Did McBride discharge his pistol on the street where there were innocent bystanders?”

“Well, yeah, but . . .”

Before Byers could continue, Flynn looked at McBride and said, “Okay, smart-ass, we got you now. You’re under arrest for being negligent, ignoring procedures, and firing a gun into a crowd. Why are you wearing your badge?” Flynn motioned to an officer standing nearby and said, "Take his badge and put him in lockup."

"He has witnesses that say he did not ignore procedures and was careful about firing his gun," Byers said.

"Hell, witnesses are never reliable in these situations. The DA can breakdown witnesses, and he'll believe whatever we tell him," Flynn said and gave Patrick a hard look. "Your friend, old Judge Webster, won't be able to save your ass now. We can get rid of you for good."

Lieutenant Byers signaled Flynn to stop, but he ignored him.

"McBride has a credible witness. I witnessed the entire scene, and he did nothing wrong. I'm willing to testify to that," District Attorney Robert Ingraham said.

"So, you're a witness. Why don't you take your witness shit and leave? I don't want to hear it."

"I think you'll want to hear what I have to say, Chief Flynn. The DA will not break down my testimony because I'm district attorney Robert Ingraham. As I tried to tell you, this officer followed the procedures, *your* procedures, to the letter. Now, what did you say about getting rid of this officer?"

Flynn looked surprised, but recovered quickly. "I was funning young McBride," he said. "Why he's one of the best patrolmen on the force. I don't doubt he'll be promoted to detective before the year is out. All the merchants on his beat sing his praises. Since he came on the beat, shoplifting is down ninety percent. Why would I want to get rid of an exemplary officer? Give McBride's badge back. Where is his weapon, Byers?"

"I gave it to desk sergeant."

"Well, give it back. There will no need for a review," said Flynn. "I knew a new district attorney was coming but didn't know you were here already. Welcome to the Memphis Police Department, Mr. Ingraham."

Byers told a clerk to retrieve Patrick's gun.

"Thanks, Chief Flynn. I'll be seeing a lot of you. And, I will take a special interest in McBride. He showed a lot of discipline in a tense situation." The DA said to Patrick, "Come by my office for a chat. There may be a place for a detective in the DA's office."

"Yes, sir."

Ingraham gave the chief and sergeant a dismissive wave of his hand and left. When the DA was out of sight, the chief gave Patrick a deadly look, slammed the door angrily and went into his office.

Lieutenant Byers shook his head and walked toward his desk leaving Patrick standing. The clerk handed him the gun. He was still holding his pistol in front the chief's door when Sergeant Flaherty walked up.

"You waiting to get your ass handed to you? Are you going to holster that piece or not?"

"Chief Flynn and Lieutenant Byers just left me here, so am I off duty? If so, I'm going home."

"I heard you used your weapon today. Why do you have it now? It hasn't been long enough for a review of the shooting."

"There will be no hearing or review. Chief Flynn gave my gun back and said no review."

"Well, I'll be a monkey's uncle. Flynn did that? Why?"

"My witness to the shooting, District Attorney Ingraham, had a little to do with it," said Patrick.

"Ingraham? I didn't know he had taken over from John Matthews, that crook, even Boss Crump couldn't save Matthews from jail time."

"Detective sergeant Bill Bonner took him down for selling light sentences to criminals for the right amount of money. City hall won't interfere with the new DA. The desk sergeant already sent someone to cover for your patrol. Go on home and relax. You've had enough excitement for one day. I'll hear your story later. Enjoy your good fortune as long as you can," Flaherty said.

"Is that why Detective Bonner is on the chief's shit list?"

"You guessed it. McBride, you're damn lucky. Just remember, someday there won't be any coincidences. A judge or district attorney or the cavalry won't show up to save your ass."

"I won't need a coincidence. I'll always have you, Sergeant Flaherty," Patrick said. He heard the sergeant scoff as he walked away.

When Patrick stepped outside the police station door, Laura Hemphill grabbed him and hugged and kissed him hard.

"Damn you, Patrick McBride. I was scared to death. I heard a holdup man shot a policeman at Piggly-Wiggly on Second Street, and I thought it could be you. Nobody would tell me anything at the desk. I had to wait around here making a fool out of myself and crying, before Albert Sidney came out and said you were okay, and you were the one that shot a robber."

"You're my lucky charm, Laura. Come with me. I need something to settle my nerves."

"Me, too."

Patrick never noticed her concern was more than that of a good friend. That night he wrote to the McMasters and softened the description of the shooting as if it were routine. When they read the account in the *Knoxville Journal*, they knew he is trying to keep them from worrying.

CHAPTER 15

ONE MORE SESSION

By March 1923, the courts gave the Bandon children nothing to encourage them to continue protesting the colonel's will. The two Bandons claimed Elizabeth Formstone had seduced their uncle and influenced him to write them out of the will. Friends of the Formstones were aware of his wishes and testified that the colonel had all his faculties until his dying day. Colonel Bishop, who had served with Formstone in the Shropshire Light Infantry, told the hearing that he had witnessed the will and Mrs. Formstone hadn't been present and didn't know the contents of the will until long after he, Colonel Bishop, witnessed it.

In June 1923, Colonel Formstone's niece and nephew tried hiring their fourth solicitor. Solicitors heard of their proclivity for ignoring lawyer's advice and declined to take their case. A worn-out James Bledsoe took their case on speculation. The legal fees depleted their bank accounts, and they had second thoughts about settling for whatever amount negotiated.

Banny insisted on being present at the table when Bledsoe talked with Beth's lawyers about what she would give up.

Ralph Hawkins went straight to the point. "Mr. Bledsoe, we tried to settle this matter months ago by offering one hundred thousand pounds to each litigant. They refused our offer."

"Yeah. We refused because it wasn't enough. We want a million pounds each," Banny said.

"Please, Mr. Bandon. Let me do the negotiating," Bledsoe said.

"You're a thief, Bledsoe. As far as I know, you and Hawkins

colluded to earn a big, fat fee. We'll not take less than a million pounds each," Banny said.

"We have nothing to negotiate. Good day, sir," Hawkins said and carefully placed his notes and papers in his briefcase. "We were prepared to offer four hundred thousand each. Now, it will be a cold day in hell before you get a dime. We'll see you in court." Hawkins and Kelly rose from the table and started toward the door.

"Mr. Bandon, you find another lawyer that will work on speculation. I quit," Bledsoe said.

"Wait. Wait. Maybe I'm a little hasty in my assessment of the situation. Let us sit and talk," Banny said.

"When you begin to make sense, I'll ask Mrs. Formstone what she wants to do. I will recommend going to court. The colonel's will is ironclad, and no one will ever break it. You better believe me. Mrs. Formstone offered a cash settlement out of the goodness of her heart. Goodbye, Mr. Bandon," Hawkins said.

"Goodbye, Mr. Bandon," Bledsoe said.

Banny watched the three men walk through the door and dreaded what he would tell his sister. Four hundred thousand pounds each is not a laughing amount, and he had to find a way to bring the lawyers back to the table.

"The two Bandons think if they become unbearable irritants, we will give in to their unrealistic demands," said Philip.

"I'll have a friend look into their finances. If we can persuade Beth to hold out a bit longer, we'll have them," Hawkins said.

"Beth is getting very tired, and I can't blame her. She may agree to some extreme amount if she goes back into a negotiation session. I don't want her to hear what the Bandons call her. That may break her down. I try to keep up her spirits by talking to her about anything but this legal action. I think I am falling for Beth," said Philip out of the blue. "I do not want to use this feeling to keep her from giving in to those horses' asses, and yet I'm tempted."

"Philip, I can see why you are falling for that young woman. Give me back forty years I would give you a race," Hawkins said.

Before Christmas on Sunday afternoon after a light meal at Beth's house. Philip said, "Beth, it's time we thought about the future. The

Bandons will soon give up, and you will be free to marry me.”

“We’ve been through this months ago, and I have not changed my mind.”

Philip continued, “I love you, Beth, and I want you to be my wife. Will you?”

“No. I still hold out hope that Patrick and I will find each other. If he does not come back to Shrewsbury, I will go to America. I love Patrick and will not abandon hope that he will come for me. I cannot accept your proposal.”

“And if he doesn’t come?”

“I’ll search for him in America. If I do not find him, I will know I tried.”

“Just remember, I will not wait forever,” Philip Kelly replied.

CHAPTER 16

No Regrets

Having no regrets about taking a man's life and hardly remembering what had happened, bothered Patrick. His fellow officers avoided him as if he had the flu from the 1918 epidemic until they found out Chief Flynn said that there was no need for an investigation. For several weeks afterward the incident, merchants on his beat offered gifts of all sort, which he refused. Piggly-Wiggly sent a ham. Reluctantly, he sent it back. He told the merchants the city paid him to do the job and wouldn't accept gifts.

At last his fellow patrolmen congratulated Patrick for his shot.

"That's a hell of a shot from where you were standing. I didn't think you had it in you."

"Yeah. Good thing you were quick to shoot. Had the robber been a little faster, you'd be the one in the ground."

"McBride, I'll have to watch you on the range. I want you to show me how to hit a target with this Colt .45."

Although he won the respect of his fellow officers, McBride regretted that it had to be for killing a man. He finally decided to talk to someone that had experienced the same predicament. He trusted Sergeant Flaherty enough to ask his help. He overheard the sergeant tell someone he went around the corner to Big Town Billiards after work to unwind. When Patrick went off duty, he dressed in his gray suit and walked around the corner to the billiard parlor.

Law officers in every town have a hangout. In Memphis, police favored Big Town Billiards. Frenchie Piot, the owner, served sandwiches in the back room with coffee cups filled with something stronger than what they were intended for. The whiskey came in two varieties, bad or good. If you were low on money, the bad was affordable. For a little more, the alleged imported stuff wouldn't make you wish you were dead. Since it was their favorite hangout, Big Town had protection from raids by any law enforcement; even the feds stayed away.

Patrick entered through swinging doors and stood there, letting his eyes get accustomed to the dim interior. There were four pool tables with overhead lights. Shooting rotation at one of the tables were two men, wearing white dress shirts with sleeves rolled up. He couldn't tell whether they were cops or civilians. At the counter, sat a little man on a high stool which Patrick took as Frenchie.

Before Patrick said anything, Frenchie asked, "What can I do for you?"

"Is Sergeant Flaherty in the back room?"

"Haven't seen Flaherty. What do you want with him?"

"That's my business. Go tell Flaherty that McBride wants to see him."

"Hey, Bobby, go tell Flaherty he's wanted out here by a McBride."

Bobby, the man that worked for tips keeping tables clean and racking billiard balls, walked to the door marked "private" in the back of the pool room, knocked, and went in. Flaherty came out and saw Patrick.

"McBride, you're a wet blanket. I was enjoying myself," said Flaherty with a grin.

"Sorry to break up your party. I need to ask you a question in private."

The sergeant motioned to an empty row of stadium-style seats, set against the wall for patrons to watch the pool tournaments Frenchie held on Friday and Saturday nights.

"This is about as private as you can get," he said and motioned at the far end of the seats.

After they settled on the lower row, Flaherty asked, "What's on your mind?"

"Have you ever killed a man?"

The sergeant thought for a second and said, "Not on the Memphis police force. Yeah, in the war. Why?"

"What do you remember about it?"

"Not much. I don't know if it were me that got the enemy. I pointed my rifle at him and pulled the trigger. He fell, and that's about it. Never as a Memphis cop. Listen, you're one of few men who ever had to pull his weapon. Even fewer that have killed somebody."

"Killing that fellow doesn't bother me."

"I can tell you all the platitudes about forgetting and leaving it behind, but I can't help you," Flaherty said.

"That's my problem," Patrick said. "I have forgotten. I hardly remember having shot and killed a man. What can I do?"

"I know this cop that has killed a couple of times. I'll try to arrange a meet. I said, 'try.' He's not the most jovial person I know and hasn't been for a couple of years. Maybe he'll be in a rare good mood. Come in early tomorrow and see me before going on duty," Flaherty said.

"I'll be there. Thanks, sergeant."

"McBride, you owe me for setting this meeting up with Bill Bonner. He'll meet with you, but don't think you'll get a lot out of him. I honestly believe he hates everyone and everything. Don't say anything unless he asks a question. Understand."

"Okay, sergeant."

Sergeant Flaherty arranged a meet at Big Town Billiards with Bonner. Patrick stepped into the pool hall and let his eyes get accustomed to the dim pool room. He recognized Bonner from seeing him at the station. Bonner, smoking a Home Run, sat on the first row of stadium seats.

Patrick moved slowly to where he sat and said, "I'm McBride."

Bonner said nothing until he finished the cigarette, wet his fingers, and pinched fire out. He dropped the butt and smashed it on the wooden floor.

"You that smart-ass boy from back East? I don't like smart-ass boys from back East."

"If you call Kingsport, Tennessee back East, then I'm that smartass boy. And frankly, I don't give a damn whether you like me or not, I didn't come in here to make any friends."

Patrick thought he saw an almost imperceptible grin which was gone as fast as it appeared. He looked at a scar running across his left cheek and realized that hot lead made the scar. Another injury showed white in the graying hair above the right ear.

"Then, you're that smart-ass boy from Kingsport."

"Have it your way. I needed to talk to someone smarter than I. Sergeant Flaherty said you were that person. I was misinformed," Patrick said and turned to go.

"Maybe, maybe not," Bonner said before Patrick could take a step. "Flaherty said that you couldn't understand why you feel no regret for shooting scum. That right?"

"In a nutshell."

"I can't tell you. I killed Germans in France and never thought about it. But that was at a distance, and bullets were flying both ways. My first shooting as a Memphis cop took little getting used to. But I remembered he would have shot me without blinking an eye, and I forgot about killing him. There were three more since 1918, and I remember them as notches on my gun."

"You cut notches on your gun?"

"A figure of speech. All I can tell you is to work it out yourself. I know that's not what you want to hear, but that's all I can give. Except, be thankful you don't remember."

"Thanks for the talk," Patrick said.

"McBride, if you tell anyone about our little talk, you'll have my billy club upside your head," Bonner warned him.

"Don't worry about that, Detective Sergeant Bonner. I wouldn't want anybody to know I talked with you," said Patrick and quickly walked away.

This time Bonner showed a broad, crooked grin that no one saw.

Chapter 17

Belated Christmas Present

December 19, 1923
Dear Folks,

I'm sorry I can't get home for Christmas. Duty calls, especially if you are low man on the totem pole. Laura Hemphill and I will celebrate Christmas Eve. Please look for a package in the mail. Merry Christmas.

Yours,

Patrick celebrated his ninth month on the police force and Christmas with Laura Hemphill. On Christmas Eve night after they exchanged presents, Laura curled up on the sofa beside him.

"Thanks, for the lovely necklace. I think you spent too much."

"Laura, you have been a great friend to me this past year, and I've enjoyed every minute. Other than you, who else do I have to spend on?"

"I hope I've become more than just a friend."

"Maybe. I have always been honest with you. Walking a police beat is a temporary job. I don't have ambition in the police department regardless of what the Judge Otis and Emma Webster think. I'm on my way to Texas and don't want to get involved."

Laura reached over, pulled his head down, and kissed him. She hid the tears in her eyes.

"Change your mind?" she asked.

"Hard not to," he said and kissed her back. "Want to try again?"

Patrick turned on the radio and tuned to radio station WMC, and they listened to Isham Jones, Bennie Kreuger, and Bessie Smith. They danced to Paul Whiteman. They were soon back on the sofa with heavy petting. Patrick came up for air and said, "Laura, it's ten thirty. If you're going to Christmas with your family, I'll walk you home."

"Can't I stay here? I won't be any trouble. I'll behave, I promise. I'll even sleep on the sofa," she said. "And I'll be out of here early in the morning before you get ready for duty. You won't even know when I leave."

"You know better than to ask. You know how you affect me."

"I don't mean to affect you. Please, it's cold out, and I promise I won't bother you."

"Okay. I'll sleep on the sofa. You take my bedroom," Patrick said and reached a hand down to help her off the sofa.

Laura took his hand pulled him down and kissed him hard. "Take that, you old softie."

Christmas morning found Patrick up and dressed in uniform by five thirty. Trying not to wake Laura, he quietly made toast in the oven and boiled coffee in the pot. Laura came out of his bedroom wearing one of his white shirts.

"Mmmm, coffee smells good," she said. "Did you sleep well last night?"

"Not really. The sofa is bad for my back. I'm a little stiff this morning."

"You were a little stiff last night, but you wouldn't let me do anything about that. I can massage your back and make it feel better. I hope you didn't mind my wearing your shirt. You'd be embarrassed if I came out in my birthday suit."

"Laura, sometimes you make me blush, like now. That's not funny."

"It wasn't intended to be funny. It's the truth. How about some coffee?"

"Get it yourself, you hussy."

After coffee and toast, Laura went into Patrick's bedroom to get dressed. He was on his second cup.

"Patrick!" she called.

Thinking something was wrong he rushed to the bedroom door.

Laura stood holding his shirt, so it concealed her naked body.

"Do you want to put this in the dirty clothes?" Laura asked, pitched the shirt to him and slammed the door. She made sure he got the full view.

"I know what you're trying to do," he said through the bedroom door, "and it's not going to work. I'm going to Texas."

Some hidden emotion came to the surface of his mind, but not because her body was almost perfect. It was—and much better than the strippers in Germany or the French girls on nude Mediterranean beaches. He dismissed that strange feeling that it was just a one-time thing.

"Mr. McBride, you have a suspicious mind. I'm not trying to do anything."

"Then, what was that little stunt you just pulled?"

"Gee, I thought we were good friends. What's a little nudity between friends?"

"I'm going to work, you evil woman. See you soon."

The loneliest holiday of the year is Christmas Day. He thought about spending the holidays in Kingsport with the McMasters but knew he couldn't get back in time for duty on Wednesday, the day after Christmas. He volunteered to take two shifts on Christmas Day. The work would be easy since stores closed for the holiday. But McBride didn't count on snow. It started at eleven o'clock; by that afternoon there were two inches on the ground and it was still snowing. He missed Laura and thought of her every step of his patrol. They would have fun in the snow, but he knew the relationship was more than that.

Now, he was ready to admit his deep feelings. His steps were lighter as he walked his beat and checked in at the call box every hour. Streetlights didn't do much for dark corners, so he avoided walking close to stores. For this reason, he wasn't surprised when a figure came out of the dark.

"Hey, mister. You got any money. I'm hungry. Ain't had anything to eat since yesterday."

"I have two dollars. Will that do?"

"Anything you have will help out. Hey, you're a cop. I wasn't begging, honestly."

"Okay. You weren't begging. Where are you going to buy food on this holiday?"

"Big Town Billiards is open in the back room. They got sandwiches."

"And whiskey, too."

"Yes, sir. That too, but I'm too hungry to drink rotgut."

"You're wearing an army uniform. Were you in France?" Patrick asked.

"Yes, sir."

"Okay. Take the two dollars. When you get to the back room, ask for a Bill Bonner. Tell him Chief Roscoe Flynn wishes him a Merry Christmas and orders him to buy you a meal. Can you remember that?"

"Bill Bonner, Chief Flynn, buy me a meal. I can remember and will tell Bill Bonner just that. Thank you, officer."

"I hope he does. That brightens my day all ready."

Time passed by faster than Patrick thought it would. His relief came to the call box at twelve sharp. It stopped snowing, leaving three inches with the top freezing. He crunched his way to the station and quickly, changed into street clothes. He carefully brushed his uniform and dried his shoes before heading home on the rail.

I have to buy a car. Maybe a used Model T. I don't relish walking the rest of my life, he thought.

At home, he wrote to the McMasters:

Tuesday, December 25, 1923
Dear Folks,

I'm sorry I didn't make it home for Christmas. It's a lonely time without anyone with whom to celebrate. Laura went home to her folks. She will be back tomorrow, and I'm anxious to see her. I have felt this way about a girl before, and I'll find out how she feels about me tonight. I won't make the same mistake I made in Liverpool. Did you get the presents I sent? I received your gifts two days before Christmas Eve. Thanks for the Zane Grey novel and the scarf.

Yours always,

McBride had a fitful night without much sleep and woke, not as bright as usual. For the first time, he dreaded going to work. Snow had frozen, and even with the heavy coat, the cold wind cut into him like a knife on the way to the station. He greeted his fellow policemen and suited up for his beat.

"McBride, you sorry son-of-a-bitch. I should shoot you now and get it over with," Sergeant Bill Bonner shouted.

Patrick stood with a surprised and bewildered look.

"I know it was you, and it ain't funny. I'll have your head on a pole."

"What are you so riled about, sergeant?"

"Don't give me that innocent look and 'what are you so riled up about shit.' You know what damn well."

The policemen going on and off duty gathered to see what was going on.

"I only met you one time. If I have offended you in any way, Sergeant Bonner, I apologize."

Lieutenant. Byers came up fast. "Bonner, you're always making trouble. Get going before I put you on report. And you, McBride, that goes for you too."

Before he started for his beat, Sergeant Flaherty caught up with him and said, "What did you do to Bonner?"

He quickly explained what happened. They both laughed. Flaherty was still laughing when Patrick left the station. He felt much better about walking patrol, then his thoughts returned to Laura. His emotions bounced about like a rubber ball. He felt weak and then high. He realized he was in love before Albert Sidney relieved him. He wanted to talk, but Patrick told him he had to get home fast. He had to find out about Laura's feelings for him.

He opened the door to his apartment, the pleasant smell of steak and potatoes wafted through the room. His nose couldn't believe it.

"Hello, Officer McBride. Would you like a glass of wine before supper?" Laura called out from the kitchen.

Patrick dropped his overcoat on a chair before going into the kitchen.

"Laura, how did you get into my apartment?"

"You gave me a key yesterday."

"That was to lock up when you left."

"I'm sorry, Patrick. Please forgive me. I promise, it'll never happen again, I never meant to keep the key. Really. I thought you would enjoy a home-cooked meal tonight." Laura said.

"You know, I can't be angry with you. It has come to my attention that I may have to stay in Memphis and not go to Texas if circumstance permits," Patrick said.

"That's sudden. I thought you had made up your mind to go. What circumstances are you talking about?"

"If I left, you would follow me, so I'll save you the trouble," he said.

"Pretty sure of yourself, aren't you?"

"Yes, I'm staying in Memphis to marry you," he said.

She froze with a spatula in her hand and asked, "What does that mean? Is that a proposal?"

"Is it yes or no?"

Then, she pulled back, "Please don't kid me, Patrick. If you do, I'll die."

"I wouldn't kid the woman I've come to love more than Texas or anything else on this earth."

After their steak and potato supper, they had a custard dessert from the bakery.

"I don't feel like going for a moving picture now," she said. "Let's stay home and talk."

"How about the wine? Let's save it for a big celebration," he said. "I'll invite all my friends." He held up one finger.

"You know, I *would* have followed you to Texas. I fell in love with you the first time I saw you. I knew you were the one, and I'd pursue you to the ends of the earth. I have a confession to make. I didn't just run into you on Second Street that day, I searched for and found you."

"You devious woman, I'm glad you found me. And you can keep my key."

After Patrick returned from seeing Laura to her apartment, he wrote a letter to the Kingsport couple:

December 26
Dear Folks,
    I finally built up enough courage to ask Laura to marry. She agreed. I haven't given her an engagement ring. That's coming real soon. I know you will love Laura as much as I do.
        Yours,

The next day after Patrick left work, he met Laura at Lane's Fine Jewelry Store and shopped for an engagement ring. Laura looked at the rings in the showcase and chose one to see. Mr. Lane pulled out the entire tray. She picked the one she liked and asked, "How much is this one?"

"I'll sell it to you for one thousand dollars."

Laura immediately put it back on the tray and asked, "What's the price range of this tray?"

"These rings range from five hundred to one thousand," said Mr. Lane.

"These are beautiful rings, but a little out of our price range. Could I see something that costs between fifty and one hundred dollars?"

"Choose the ring you want, and I'll buy it for you," Patrick said.

Mr. Lane showed a tray with rings for fifty up to two hundred dollars.

"I like this ring, Patrick. I want this one."

"I thought you liked the one in the other tray. It's a beautiful ring and will look great on your finger."

"I agree, but I like this one better. Will you buy this for me?"

"An excellent choice, Miss Hemphill," Mr Lane said. "I know you'll be satisfied with the ring Patrick buys."

"I'll be by tomorrow on my beat and pay for it."

"Very good. Now, Miss Hemphill, let's size it."

After they left the store, Laura asked, "Do you have enough money to pay for my ring?"

"Yes. I saved up quite a bit."

"Okay, if you need some money, I also saved."

That evening they dined at Boyer's Oak Room, one of the best restaurants in Memphis. The food was excellent, and the service lived up to its reputation.

"The girls at the store are jealous. They said you'd never propose, and I love to rub it in."

"I got about the same reaction at the station. The bachelors said you were too good for me. The married guys said I was looking for a ball and chain. They also said I got one of the prettiest girls in Memphis."

The couple was having coffee after dinner when Patrick asked, "Where would you like to celebrate New Year's Eve?"

"We could stay home and celebrate there."

"I'd rather go out. Now, this is your town. Where shall we go?"

"I understand Top Hat has a great New Year's Party. James Bell's Orchestra will be there. After midnight Bill Coye's Jazz Band will finish up the night. It's not that expensive. There will be lots of free champagne."

"Will we need reservations?

"For New Year's, yes," Laura said.

"I'll make reservations tomorrow."

Patrick checked his schedule and saw he had duty on Sunday, New Year's Eve, along with four-hour extended shift the brass set up to be fair, but he was off on Monday. He didn't want to disappoint Laura but knew he would be able to make Top Hat New Year's Eve party. He asked around but could find nobody to take his extra shift.

As promised, he entered Lane's Fine Jewelry Store, and Mr. Lane met him at the jewelry showcase.

"I have your ring ready," he said and went to the back of the store and brought out a ring case. "She'll be surprised to get this thousand-dollar ring."

"You're the only person in Memphis who knows of my good fortune, and I would like to keep it that way."

"I have always been discreet about who buys what." Lane opened the box and showed the ring.

"It is beautiful. Thanks, Mr. Lane."

Patrick put the box in his pocket and began to think about when to give her a ring. She didn't leave work until five o'clock. He decided to formally propose to her with the ring in the store. He doubled timed it and made it by four fifty.

Patrick walked into the store and heard someone calling to the back of the store, "Laura, your darling sweetheart is here." Along with this came much giggling.

"Tell Laura I am here," Patrick said with a solemn look, and the giggling stopped.

"Patrick, what are you doing here? Darn you, I wanted to surprise you with a gift, but it'll have to wait."

A bystander said, "Uh-oh."

"I'll be off in about five minutes," Laura said.

"What I have to say can't wait."

Mr. Jacobs came from the back of the store, "Ladies, you still have five minutes. Give this couple some air."

"No, Mr. Jacobs, please let them stay. I want to tell Laura something and want them to be present so there will be no mistakes, afterward."

"No, Patrick, please don't," Laura begged thinking Patrick would break his proposal.

"Laura Hemphill, we are not formally engaged until you accept my ring. So, if you're sure you know what you're about to get into," he pulled the ring box from his pocket and opened it. "I love you. Will you marry me?"

"Yes," Laura said and kissed him to applause from Mr. Jacobs and the women in the store.

Patrick placed the ring on her finger, and she held her hand up and looked at it. "This is not the ring I picked out. It's the one-thousand-dollar ring I told you I didn't want."

"Your eyes shined when you looked at this ring but dimmed with disappointment when you said you wanted the cheap one. I want to see your eyes shine every day as long as we live."

"But it costs too much."

"I refuse to discuss this until we well out of the earshot of these good people."

"Get out, you two," Mr. Jacobs told them. Laura grabbed her coat, and they left holding hands.

CHAPTER 18

SETTLED IN '24

Until a settlement with the Bandons over the disputed will was reached, no one in the Hawkins firm could predict when all the colonel's bequests could be carried out. Philip Kelly predicted sometime in 1924.

Beth didn't notice that spring ended and summer slipped in without holidays or trips to the beach. She still dreamed of Patrick McBride and their time together. Philip Kelly kept her informed about the disposition of colonel's will. The Bandon siblings fired Bledsoe and hired another solicitor.

Moses Salmon, the new lawyer, started pressuring the Hawkins firm. He offered to consider two hundred thousand pounds for each of the Bandon children, as he referred to them. Solicitors Hawkins and Kelly agreed to meet, not in Birmingham, but in Salmon's Shrewsbury office without the Bandons. They met in Salmon's interoffice, and after the solicitor served tea, they started the negotiations. The door to the office flew open, and Banny Bandon came in screaming at Salmon.

"That slut screwed Uncle Gadsden to get his money. Now, you're talking to that lowlife creature's solicitors without my presence. You will not meet with anyone and talk about our inheritance. Do you understand Fish Head. I told you we wouldn't take anything less than his entire estate. So, this meeting is over."

Hawkins and Kelly closed their briefcases and left Salmon sitting at his negotiating table in stunned silence.

"What can we do if these unreasonable idiots won't talk?" Kelly asked.

"Take it to court if can get a judge to listen," Hawkins said.

The courts insist litigants settle the matter without court intervention.

"If the judge attended one of our sessions. The settlement would come forthwith."

Kelly reported to Beth the next day. "It was not a pleasant meeting. Salmon called and offered to settle for two hundred thousand pounds each. We thought it was a good starting point and agreed to the meeting without the Bandons. Before we started, Banny broke in and told Salmon to never talk about their inheritance without one of them being present. Mr. Hawkins and I believe we will have to let the court decide. However, I am confident the Bandons are too short on funds to pursue this much farther."

"I am tempted to give them half the inheritance just to have it over and done with," said Beth. "But they are so greedy; I'll be in hell before they get any more than we offer."

"Let's sweeten the pot a bit more. Maybe two hundred and fifty thousand pounds each. They have to be running short of money and will soon resort to paying contingency percentage for their solicitor," said Philip.

CHAPTER 19

MEMPHIS NEW YEAR – 1924

"So, you're rich," Laura said.

"I didn't say that. I said my dad left me enough money for us to go somewhere nice on a honeymoon and not have to pay for it later. My year is up in March, and I'll put in for vacation after we're married."

"Maybe we'll be married before March."

"That's okay. The sooner, the better. Then you'll stop bothering me with those nudity-between-friends stunts," Patrick said.

"You'll never let me live that down, will you?"

"Not in a million years," Patrick said.

"I've thought about April."

"You plan our wedding, and I'll show up sober."

"Do you mind if we have Sunday supper at Mother's. She wants to meet you."

"I'm sorry, Laura. I planned to tell you that I have a shift and a half on Sunday. I'll have to decline the dinner invitation, and the New Year's Eve party at Top Hat is off. It will be too late by the time I get home. I'll have New Year's Day off. Could we go to your mother's on Monday?"

"Where are we going New Year's Eve after you get off from work? askcd Laura.

"We'll just have to stay at home, I guess."

"May I use your—my—key?

"You can use either one you want. Make sure you return one next year."

He had no duty on Saturday, so he caught the Memphis Rail to the Buick dealership on Union Street. Patrick walked on the car lot and a salesman, wearing a baggy black overcoat, white shirt, and a yellow poka-dot bowtie, was on him like a cat on a mouse.

"You ready to buy a car that will flat out run?" He stuck out his hand and gave Patrick a big, toothy smile. "I'm T. Earl Dollar, and I've got a deal for you. The finest motorcar you'll ever own is a Cadillac. Yes, sir . . ."

"Hold on. I'm not interested in a Cadillac. Show me another model."

"You look like you know your automobiles. We have this 1922 Marmon Sedan. It's new, but the 1923s came out and left us high and dry with 1922. We need to move it. You can drive this beauty out for a mere three thousand and eight hundred dollars. Now, we can set up a payment plan that will not cost you a cent in interest for the first two weeks."

"This car ready to drive, T. Earl?"

"Yes, sir. get behind the wheel and start her up with the electric starter."

"I'll take it."

"Let's go to the office and fill out some papers. We'll give you a bill of sale and fix a payment schedule."

"Will you sell it for a flat three thousand dollars if I pay cash?"

T. Earl hesitated for a minute and asked, "You got cash on you now? You got yourself a deal."

An hour later Patrick drove out of the dealership in a new 1922 Marmon sedan. He had to get accustomed to driving the Marmon, which was more advanced than the Model T Ford.

He drove outside of town and on a country road to get to know the workings better. He had to limber it up and found the gear shift was hard to operate until he shifted without the clutch. He parked the new car in a space he'd had the apartment owners fix. He wanted to show Laura but had to wait for her to leave work.

At four thirty he caught the rail to Madison Avenue and waited for Laura outside Jacob's Department Store. She came out at five and began walking in deep thought toward the rail stop. He fell into step with her and said, "Come home with me and we'll make mad love."

"Patrick, you'll give me a heart attack someday."

"Will you come home with me, anyway. You can talk about our wedding."

They caught the rail to his apartment. She saw the Marmon powder-gray sedan in the parking space. "Do you know who owns that car? It's beautiful."

"I do. Want to go for a spin? It has an excellent heater, like we'll need one."

"You're such a fibber, Patrick McBride. How can I ever believe you?"

He took her hand and led her to the car, opened the passenger door, and said, "Hop in, Doubting Laura."

She still didn't believe it until he started the engine and pulled out of the parking space.

"Do you think we can go in the Marmon to your mother's on Monday?"

"You are a devil. You didn't tell me you were going to buy a motorcar."

"I thought about it but couldn't decide until our engagement. After we're married, we'll need transportation other than walking or rail. I want to picnic in the country come Spring. We may take this on our honeymoon if it's short."

"How did you pay for this? I know it wasn't cheap."

"My dad left me a little money."

Patrick parked in his space and opened the door for Laura.

"Well, it's your money."

They sat in their usual places, she cuddled up to him, on the sofa in his apartment. "Sweetheart, you'll know this after we're married, so I might as well tell you now," Patrick said.

Here it comes, she thought.

"I have a trust worth over a quarter-million-dollars. I draw five thousand a year. And live on what I make as a policeman and save the rest. I've put that in a banking account."

"You're not joking, are you?"

"I wanted you to have your engagement ring. I felt we needed the car."

She cuddled closer and kissed him, "I would love you if you didn't have a cent."

CHAPTER 20

DINNER AT MOTHER'S

Sunday found Patrick and Laura sitting at her mother's table with ten of her extended family. Every one of them asked where he was from, what he did, where they would be married, and whether they were they coming back to Germantown to live after they were married.

He told them about patrolling a small part of Memphis and said that Laura made the wedding plans. Uncle Harry Douglas talked cars and Patrick took him for a ride in the Marmon.

"Woo-wee, that's some powerful motorcar. It would suck my Model T up the exhaust," he said.

When they got ready for the drive back to Memphis, Laura's mother put some of her fantastic fried chicken in a container for Patrick's dinner on Tuesday.

"Patrick, you'll have to come back when peaches come in. I'll make you a pie," her mother told him.

"You bet I will."

The men and boys shook his hand, and the ladies and girls pecked him on the cheek. All ten family members and a couple of neighbors waved goodbye when the tired couple left for the hour's drive to Memphis.

"You made a hit with my family," Laura said.

"It looks as if they have a place for us to live. Beautiful, rich farmland. Harry Douglas said he would talk to the sheriff about a job for me. His wife is the sheriff's cousin, ya know. His deputy's pay is pretty good too. I enjoyed every minute of this short stay. It's good for me to experience a large family since I never had one."

"Would you live in Germantown?" Laura asked.

"I love you enough to live where you want."

The following weekends, when Patrick wasn't on the duty roster, were spent visiting Judge Otis and Emma Webster. Emma told the judge in front of them that many times her Cupid meddling pays off. He scoffed.

Albert Sidney and Patrick were off at the same time and finally had the double date they planned weeks ago. Patrick didn't say so, but Laura had no competition from Albert Sidney's girlfriend.

It was a heady time for the engaged couple, and if it were possible, they became more in love and more devoted to each other. Patrick didn't mind patrolling Court Avenue; he knew Laura would be waiting for him to pick her up in the Marmon. She became a fixture in his apartment complex, but always reluctantly let Patrick take her home. She didn't pull more "What's a little nudity between friends" stunts. They weren't friends anymore.

On Monday after St. Valentine's Day, Sergeant Flaherty told Patrick that he could go to his duty station late because District Attorney Ingraham wanted to see him in his office. Patrick sat in the waiting room until the DA's secretary told him to go in.

Ingraham rose to greet him when he entered the office. "Patrick, I'm glad to see you. I was determined to take Flynn down a couple of notches. He sure did try to crab out of the situation."

"Yes, sir. Chief doesn't speak to me, and I'm still on his list."

"I'll get right to the point. I need a detective on staff, and you are the one I want."

"Mr. Ingraham, I have no experience. There are others in the police department that have many years of experience."

"You have three years at an Ivy League school. That's no small accomplishment and after a few hours of training, you can do the job. The salary is better than starting in the department. I heard you are engaged to be married. You'll be home almost every night. It's your job if you want it."

"That's a terrific offer, Mr. Ingraham. It's no secret that I started out for Texas before I got off track in Memphis. I've not completely given up on my plan. Let me think about it for a couple of days. I'll give my answer by the end of next week."

Patrick went back to the squad room and checked in with Sergeant Flaherty.

"What did the DA want?" Asked the sergeant.

"He offered me a staff detective job."

"And?"

"I told him I would give him an answer next week," Patrick answered.

"Don't wait. Take it now," the sergeant said.

"I want to talk to Laura. I haven't given up on going to Texas. If she doesn't want to leave Memphis, I'll take it."

Patrick suited up to relieve the Patrolman Benton who in his absence covered his beat. He went to the desk sergeant, "It will take five minutes to relieve Benton. I'll call when I get to Court Street."

"Chief wants to see you now. Forget about relieving Benton."

Patrick passed Sergeant Flaherty on his way back to Chief Flynn's office. Flaherty asked by facial expression, and Patrick answered by shrugging his shoulders.

Patrick stopped at the secretary's desk. She gave him a big smile and said, "Go in. Chief Flynn and Lieutenant Byers are waiting."

"Thank you."

Flynn sat behind his desk with many folders spread out on top. Byers stood a small distance behind the Chief.

"Sit down, McBride. Lieutenant Byers and I have gone over your record. You are a four zero officer. A perfect score on your evaluation. Strictly by the book. The merchants on your beat, rate you top drawer. Lieutenant Byers and I have decided you should have a position as detective. We've cleared your promotion with the police commissioner. We'll bring you in at one grade higher than a rookie. Can't beat that. Effective immediately. We want an answer before you leave this office," Flynn pushed his chair back and waited.

"I don't know what to say. Two offers in one day," Patrick said.

"I know about the DA. You'll get more action here, due to caseload. You want the job or not."

Acting on impulse Patrick said, "I'll take it."

"You will start in the morning. Report to Chief of Detectives

Roberts. He'll assign you to a more experienced partner. Do you have any questions? No? Take the rest of the day off. And McBride."

"Sir?"

"You can't back out. The police commissioner has tied you to the police department."

Chief Flynn and Lieutenant Byers chuckled when McBride left. "Saddling McBride with Bonner is genius," Flynn said to Byers. "They deserve each other. Maybe we'll kill two birds with one stone if they both resign in disgust. Good riddance."

Patrick walked into the squad room where Flaherty waited.

"Flynn offered me a detective job at one grade higher than a rookie. I took it."

"Bad mistake, McBride. He hired you to get back at the DA, and he'll hang you out to dry. I hate to see a good cop get screwed."

"I'll be assigned a partner tomorrow."

"Good luck. I'll be around, if I can do anything for you in the future."

Patrick went through his clothes closet and chose three suits that were not new but well-kept to wear detecting. He wanted desperately to tell Laura but had to wait for lunch. After a good brushing, he put his patrolman's uniform in the closet along with his walking shoes that showed wear on the heels.

"I am now a detective, Laura."

"Is that good or bad?"

"I got a raise."

"Is that good or bad and don't be so evasive," she said.

"I don't know yet, but I hope it will be okay. I may have to work longer hours. But between cases, I will have a lot of downtime. If you think this will make you unhappy, I'll quit Memphis police and go to work for the sheriff in Germantown."

"Will this affect our wedding plans?"

"You're not going to get off that easy, sweetheart," he said.

"I want to be with you as much as I can, and I'll be jealous of the time you spend on the job. What worries me most is your safety. So please be careful."

"Detective work is more about asking questions and solving crimes, not facing a criminal shooting a gun."

CHAPTER 21

MEET YOUR NEW PARTNER

Patrick arrived early and found Chief of Detectives Roberts at his desk on the side of the detective squad room.

"Chief Roberts, I'm Patrick McBride, and I'm new at this. Where and how do detectives check-in?"

"What did you do to Chief Flynn for him to order such a lousy assignment?

"He promoted me to detective. Is that a bad assignment?"

"It is if he orders Bill Bonner to partner with you."

Patrick remained silent for a minute or two. "Oh, well, he'll be just as excited to partner with me as I am to partner with him."

Bonner came into the squad room and looked at Chief Roberts.

"Flynn wants to see you, Bonner. He's waiting."

Bonner said nothing but gave Patrick an intense look and strolled down to Chief Flynn's office.

"Okay, what did I do wrong this time?" Bonner asked when he entered the office.

"Nothing this time, but I won't stop watching you." Flynn said. "Bonner, I found a man that's not afraid to partner up with you. His name is Patrick McBride; he just made detective."

"You never learn. I don't need a partner, especially him, and don't want one. Odds are this worm won't last two weeks with me."

"You'll take McBride and like it. I'm tired of your lordly ways, and you better not do anything to piss me off if you don't want to lose that pension."

"Yes sir, Chief Flynn. Anything for you, sir. You'll have no trouble from me unless I find more crooks in high places."

"Get out, Bonner. Get out and don't come back."

Patrick, waiting with Chief Roberts, heard Bonner stomp down the hallway from Flynn's office. He looked at McBride.

"High and mighty Roscoe Flynn saddled me with you. A man who stabs the very one that tries to help him. I tell you straight out; I don't like working with a partner, especially rookies. And I will not like working with you." He let out a groan. "Might as well get started. I assume you know enough to get a piece and one of them new-fangled shoulder holsters."

McBride nodded in the affirmative.

"Next payday, buy a personal piece and hope you never have to use either one. How about a typewriter? Do you know how to use a typewriter?"

"No, sir."

"Good. I don't either, and we don't have stenographers. After every shift before you go off duty, if you ever do, fill out an activity report on that typewriter using these forms."

He handed McBride a stack of forms and pointed to a new Remington typewriter that McBride had seen but never touched.

"Put the finished reports in this box marked 'Police Reports.' I doubt anybody ever reads them, but one of these days some pissant police clerk will come in and ask to see your paperwork for the past twenty years," Bonner said and paused to look at McBride. "Your training will be following me around and keeping me supplied with cigarettes and coffee. Don't—I repeat, don't—ever call me Wild Bill."

"Yes, sir."

"And don't call me 'sir.' One other thing—I don't work shifts. I stay with a case until I close it or put it in cold case files. If you can't take my schedule, you can put in for reassignment. And if you're married, you might as well tell your old lady that you'll see her some-time in the future," Bonner said. He wet his index finger and thumb, pinched the end off the fire-end of a Home Run, and pitched the butt into a trash can.

The first few weeks McBride followed Bonner around and began to think that leaving the beat was a mistake. Pulling night duty bored him because nothing ever happened. They investigated two robberies and one murder. Bonner solved the burglaries quickly because he knew every snitch and fence in Memphis.

Patrick missed Laura more than he ever thought he would. Bonner kept him late and expected him to be early for the morning shift.

Their next murder case was cut and dried. An out-of-town whiskey dealer moved into territory controlled by Benny Kerns, a local distributor. Kearns shot the outsider through the heart and left him dying outside a gin joint. Bonner intimated two witnesses into identifying the shooter. It rained that day, so the two detectives wore tan trench coats, when they caught up with Benny at the Red Lantern, a hangout for railroad workers.

Bonner looked around the bar and paused to stare at a well-dressed, handsome older man with silver hair. The man sat in a booth with a young girl whispering in her ear.

"Hubert Jakes! That bastard is back in town," the detective sergeant said out loud.

"What was that?" Patrick asked and looked at the man and girl Bonner saw.

"There's Benny Kearns at the back table with three men. Stand in the shadows a few feet behind me, kid. But don't touch your gun," Bonner said. Then, he shouted, "Hey, Benny. I got a warrant for your arrest."

The room went silent, and the three men at Benny's table slid their chairs back and broke for the door. Kearns stood up and reached for a pistol stuck in the waistband of his trousers.

"Don't do it," Bonner said in a conversational tone. "Keep your hands where I can see them or my partner will cut you down with both barrels of his shotgun. He's crazy and believe me; he's anxious to kill somebody today."

"All right, all right," Kearns said and raised his hands above his head.

"Crazy McBride. He's crazy." Bonner took the gun, handcuffed him and led him to the Model T police car. After he put the suspect inside the car, he said, "Draw your gun, kid, and keep watch on Benny. I'll be back in two shakes of a lamb's tail. Got to see someone inside."

He went back inside the Red Lantern. After a few minutes, he came out with a grim face. "You drive, kid."

McBride's hands shook as he manipulated the clutch through the gears. Now, he knew why Bonner got his nickname but decided not to tell anyone at the police station about his experience. Bonner looked back at the handcuffed Kearns.

"You just saved your own life, Benny," Bonner said. "If you confess, you aren't gonna do much time in stir for killing a bootlegger. You'll be out in no time to pursue your life of crime."

"He didn't have a shotgun, did he?"

"My partner always carries a sawed-off shotgun slung under his topcoat. He hides it because the department frowns on scatterguns, and as I told you, he's crazy. Ole crazy McBride. That's what all the cops call him."

After the detectives put Kearns in lockup, they went back to the office.

"Why did you tell Kearns I had a shotgun?"

"Within two days, every petty criminal in Memphis will know about Crazy McBride and his shotgun. It may keep you out of trouble in the future." Bonner pointed to the stack of report forms and the typewriter. "My fingers are arthritic. You write the report."

McBride started to protest but thought better of it. He hunted and pecked out the report, and after thirty minutes gave it to Bonner. "Did you know the man with the girl at Red Lantern."

Bonner didn't answer right away. "No. I thought it was Hubert Jakes. It wasn't. If it had been Jakes, I would have shot him on the spot."

"What did he do to you?" McBride asked.

"He murdered a pretty girl. A very nice girl."

"Was she kin to you?"

"No. I knew Sally and loved her. Jakes enticed her and made big promises. He murdered her to collect on a life insurance policy."

"Why didn't you arrest him for murder?"

"I couldn't prove it at that time."

Bonner looked at the report Patrick had given him and said, "Why, that's real good, kid. You sure have a knack for typing. I may get used to having you as a partner after all." He showed an evil grin, "We did our job today. Flynn will probably call us out for going into

Red Lantern, but before he does, you go home and rest or whatever. My poor arthritic fingers hurt and I'm going to the drugstore for medicine. We run night shift tomorrow. I see you at roll call."

CHAPTER 22

SERGEANT BILL BONNER

Detective Sergeant Bill Bonner joined Memphis law enforcement after he came back from The Great War in 1918. Merchants liked affable young patrolman Bill Bonner, who considered himself extremely lucky to come out of the war whole. He went out of his way to help merchants and always supported the veterans with their needs if he had the means. He built a reputation as an honest, hardworking policeman. Promotion to detective came early due to an uncanny ability to solve crimes. His interrogation technique was textbook perfect.

Something happened in 1920 that turned the affable detective Bonner into a hardened, cynical cop. He alienated his friends and kept any new policeman at a distance. One time a former friend asked, "What's happen to you, Bill? Whatever it is, I want to help."

"Keep you goddamn nose out of my business and stay away from me."

After a month or two, his partner begged Chief Flynn for a new partner or a transfer. Bonner acted as if he had a death wish and put himself in danger for no reason, and didn't care if he exposed his partner to the same risk.

"He's crazy as hell. I refuse to work with Wild Bill," his last partner told the chief.

Other detectives felt the same and refused to work with him, so the chief told Bonner to work alone until he found someone not afraid of his dangerous ways. Bonner preferred it that way and did all he could to keep from being assigned another partner. Chief Flynn tried several times to fire him, but Bonner pleased the police commissioner. The chief had to keep him.

It was in April 1920 when he fell in love with Sally Hurst. Bonner was eating breakfast in the Meridian Café near his apartment when she came in with a girlfriend. All eating stations were full at that time of the morning, so he invited the two girls to sit at his table.

"I'm Bill Bonner," he said when they settled in their chairs.

"My name is Sally Hurst, and this is Lydia Morgan."

"What brings you ladies out this early?" He had directed the question to Sally, the pretty one.

"We teach at Philips Street Grammar School," Lydia answered.

"Are you new in Memphis?" He asked.

"We're from Collierville. What kind of work do you do?" Sally asked.

"Police work. I'm an investigator for the Memphis Police Department."

"How interesting. And what do you investigate?" Sally's smile hooked him.

Bonner told them about the cases he worked. He talked to keep them at his table, to look at Sally. He forgot about his breakfast and kept talking until Sally laughed and interrupted his story.

"We really must go, Mr. Bonner, or we'll be late on our first day at a new school. Thank you for those wonderful stories."

"Will I see you again? May I see you again?" He asked, ignoring Lydia.

"If you come here for breakfast tomorrow," Sally said.

Bill Bonner had never been much of a talker to pretty girls and couldn't believe how he handled the conversation with Sally . . . like a real gentleman. That night he went home and looked in the mirror.

He had this ugly scar on his cheek where a bullet missed the vital part of his head. The white place where he parted his hair wasn't attractive, but it wasn't bad. His six-foot frame carried a small pinch of fat around the middle. In his younger days, women always commented about his strawberry blond hair, and with pride, he kept it clean and neatly cut.

His war experience plus thirteen years in the army aged him. He was still young at thirty-six but appeared older with thinning, washed-out hair. Sally Hurst was much younger. He couldn't help but wonder if she thought he was an old man.

He was smitten and realized it. Sally wasn't like the good-time girls he took out, and as a police detective, he encountered more than he wanted. Sally was a lady, and he wasn't about to screw up by coming on too strong.

Bonner religiously ate breakfast with Sally until he thought the time was right to move to the next level in their relationship.

"Sally, Sunday is my day off. Would you like to picnic at Overton Park that afternoon?"

"Yes, I've never been there. You want me to fix chicken or something?"

"If you'd like to or I can get something from the Meridian," Bonner said

"Don't be silly. I can cook fried chicken that's a lot better than the Meridian. You bring something to drink . . . ice tea . . . lemonade. Do they sell ice at the park?"

Bonner picked Sally up in his Model T and drove to Overton Park. He felt like a sixteen-year-old on his first date. He hoped he would bump into one or two of his friends so that he could show Sally off. They spread a blanket on the grass and broke out the cold chicken, biscuits and cold tea.

"I like being with you," Bonner said. "You're a beautiful person inside and out, and I'd love to spend more time with you."

"Oh, Bill. You are sweet, and I like you a lot, but I'm not ready for a permanent relationship. I want to work for a while before choosing a life mate. I hope I don't hurt your feelings."

Bonner knew what she meant. "Of course, but I'd like to take you out sometimes."

"And you can. I don't want to hurt you by having you think we have something going on."

"Then, I'll wait until you're ready." Bonner realized he rushed things but felt he still had a chance to win her heart. He couldn't give up on the best thing that had ever happened to him.

Sally and Bill continued having breakfast at the Meridian Café. They dined at Memphis' best restaurants, saw silent movies at the Majestic Theatre and even attended a play at Hopkins Opera House.

There were times Sally begged off by saying she had other commitments. The detective in Bonner wanted to follow her but resisted the urge.

One morning Sally didn't show up for breakfast with Lydia. Bonner sat at a window booth and motioned for Lydia to join him.

"Good morning, Lydia," he said when she slid into the seat across from him.

"Hi, Bill."

"Is Sally sick?"

Lydia looked at him sadly. "No, she's not. I told Sally she should tell you, but she couldn't face you."

"What are you talking about?" Bonner held his breath.

"Hubert Jakes asked her to marry and gave her a ring last night. God, Bill. I hate this. You're a better man, and I don't like him. But he's older and quite handsome and . . ." Lydia's voice drifted off into space.

"I love Sally, and I hope she finds happiness with this Jakes fellow." Bonner gritted his teeth to keep from crying. He took fifty cents out of his pocket and laid it on the table for the breakfast he had not touched.

"So long, Lydia," he said.

Detective Bonner went through police reports to see if Jakes had a record. What he found made him sick. Jakes had been married and divorced before he met Sally. Jakes had beaten his wife and put her in the hospital. The court had sentenced him to six months on a chain gang for his effort. He didn't have a job but had money and lived well. According to a report, a uniformed officer suspected Jakes was a pimp for high-price prostitutes but couldn't prove it.

Bonner wanted desperately to tell Sally what he found out about her new husband but decided to stay away. He knew she wouldn't believe him.

Six months later, Lydia called Bonner at the police station.

"Bill, Sally is bad sick. She's hurting, and I don't know what to do."

"Call a doctor. I'll be there in ten minutes," he said. Bonner rushed to the apartment as fast as his Model T could go.

Lydia met him at the door, and he heard Sally screaming.

"Did Jakes do this to her? Where is that son of a bitch?"

"He left two hours ago to do some business. Dr. Samuels, her doctor, is on his way."

Bonner entered the bedroom filled with neighbor women. Sally was in too much pain to talk, but her eyes pleaded with him to do something. But he could only hold her hand.

Dr. Louis Samuels arrived. He received his medical degree and license from the medical board two years before treating Sally. He had built his practice by giving his patients service other doctors wouldn't and didn't press for payment of bills.

The remnants of the 1917 Spanish flu epidemic still flared up in 1921. Sally's symptoms were consistent with the virus, and Dr. Samuel's diagnosed the flu. He was wrong because this wasn't the flu. In his short practice, he had not seen any person who had been poisoned and never thought any patient could ingest a lethal dose of a toxic substance.

He took Sally's hand and saw discolored nails. From the back of his mind, he dredged up what symptoms a poison victim suffered: diarrhea and discoloration of fingernails.

"She's been poisoned," the doctor said. "What have you taken, Sally? Did you take arsenic? Where did you get it?"

She tried to say something but died before she could speak.

Dr. Samuels panicked and began to gather the medicine bottles on the side table. "I need to examine these bottles. There has to be some explanation to where Sally got the arsenic."

The policeman in Bonner kicked in. "Leave the bottles," he ordered.

"I'm going back to my office. I've got to think," said the doctor and left.

A few minutes later Jakes came in shouting, "Oh, my poor Sally. Oh, my poor wife. What has he done to you? I'm going to kill that doctor. He poisoned her."

Bonner grabbed him by the shoulders and screamed, "Where the hell have you been, you bastard?"

"Do your duty, Detective Asshole. Arrest Samuels," Jakes said glaring at him.

Bonner went alone to arrest the doctor at his office above the drugstore. He parked the Model T, walked up a flight of stairs to Dr. Samuel's office. Bonner opened the door marked Dr. Louis Samuels, MD. He was shocked to see the doctor leaning over a desk with his head on his arms crying. The only time he's seen a grown man cry was in the war, and that had been over a dead horse.

"Come on, doctor. I have to take you in," he said reluctantly.

"I didn't kill Sally. I gave her a small amount of laudanum to ease the pain. I don't know how she got the arsenic. God help me, I've lost a patient."

"Doctor, get a good law—"

Before Bonner finished, Samuels raised his head off his arms. He had a gun in his right hand, and he put it to his temple and blew his brains out. After Samuels' death, there was no autopsy performed on Sally.

At Sally's funeral, Bonner watched Jakes playing the sad widower. He cried and carried on about how Samuels had poisoned his dear wife. The family buried Sally in the family plot at Collierville.

Bonner and Lydia were standing together at the burial service when Lydia whispered, "I need to tell you something."

The two walked to the edge of the cemetery and watched Jakes drive away in a sporty Model T roadster.

"It's embarrassing to have to tell you this," Lydia began. "Hubert Jakes tried to get Sally to sleep with men for money. Said he was broke and needed cash to pay off a gambling debt. She refused, and he beat her up. Bill, I urged her to call you, but she just couldn't. Just after that, she came down with the flu."

"I'm going to kill him," Bonner said. He tried to catch Jakes before he left the cemetery but wasn't fast enough. He was gone. A week later he saw Jakes in a new Cadillac driving around Memphis with a woman of questionable reputation. An ongoing investigation kept Bonner from following him.

Bonner knew Jakes didn't have money for a new car, so he began poking around to find out from where the money had come from. He hoped to find Jakes mixed up with some illegal activity but found nothing. One day he picked up a police flyer and read about a murder for life insurance money.

He began to cultivate local insurance agents for information. His search paid off when he found the agent who had sold Jakes a $10,000 life insurance policy on Sally. The insurance company had paid off and Jakes disappeared from Memphis. In his mind, Bonner went over the circumstances of Sally's death again and again. He remembered Jakes rushing into the bedroom screaming, "He poisoned her." Jakes couldn't have known that Sally died of arsenic poisoning.

"Someday I'll kill Jakes," Bill Bonner promised. He blamed himself for Sally's death and became bitter. His personality changed to not caring whether he lived or died; nor did he care about his partner's safety. The only thing that kept him alive was his determination to find and kill Hubert Jakes. For years, Jakes didn't come back to the city. Bonner gave up his search, suspecting Jakes wouldn't show his face again in Memphis.

But unbeknownst to Bonner, he did come back. Jakes was working his scams from a house on Mill Street.

CHAPTER 23

LAURA'S FLU

Patrick rushed out of the police station, and parked the Marmon in front of Jacobs Department Store and waited for Laura to come out, as was her custom. Mr. Jacobs came out and told him that Laura felt tired and left word she would be at his apartment. He called to her when he opened the apartment door. No one answered. He found her in his bed, sound asleep, and decided not to wake her.

Laura woke at nine o'clock after sleeping four hours. Patrick sat reading Zane Grey's *To the Last Man* when she came in with a yawn.

"Hello, sweetheart. Do you feel rested now?" Patrick asked.

"What time is it?" She asked.

"Nine-fifteen."

"Don't tell me I've slept that long. I guess I didn't sleep well last night. Have you had supper?"

"No, I waited for you, knowing you would be hungry when you woke up. And, you are so beautiful when you're sleeping." Patrick said.

She sat on the sofa beside him. "I'm sorry. You shouldn't have waited. I snore. You won't think I'm beautiful when you hear me snore."

He kissed her on the cheek. "You have a fever. Hope it's not catching. What would you like to eat? I can fix eggs. My specialty."

"I'm not hungry. You eat, I'm still tired."

He took her in his arms and said, "I'll hold you while you sleep."

She fell asleep almost immediately, and he carried her to his bed. Patrick finished *To the Last Man* and went to sleep on the sofa. He woke the next morning at six thirty, made coffee. He waited until seven before he knocked on the bedroom door and asked if she were decent.

"Laura, it's seven. I'll have breakfast ready in about ten minutes," he said and listened for her answer. He opened the door and saw her outside the sheet and covered with sweat. He sat on the edge of the bed and felt her forehead. It was burning fire. He tried to wake her with a kiss. It didn't work. He didn't have a phone in his apartment but used the apartment manager's phone to call a doctor and checked in with Chief of Detectives Roberts. He had the duty that night and explained he could be late. He left Bonner the message and decided he would call Mr. Jacobs at nine o'clock. Then he settled down to wait for the doctor.

Doctor Lynn knocked on the door at eight forty-five.

"What are your wife's symptoms?" he asked.

"We are engaged. Laura's family lives in Germantown. I'll take care of her here. Her symptoms are high fever, tired, weak and no appetite."

"Sounds like the flu, but I can tell you more after my examination," said the doctor.

"I thought the flu had disappeared from the United States."

"Some types of flu never disappear, and the 1918 flu is still around."

I'll try to wake her." Patrick knocked and heard some stirring from inside. "Laura, honey, I called Dr. Lynn. He is coming into the bedroom to see if he can help."

Laura hoarsely said "Okay."

Patrick opened the door and followed the doctor into the bedroom.

"Have you called Mr. Jacobs?" she asked.

"I'll call after doctor leaves."

Dr. Lynn took her temperature, listened to her heart and looked the throat and said, "Just as I thought," he said. "She has a case of the flu. Plenty of rest will do more than the medicine I am prescribing. Make sure she eats soup until she can take solid food. Miss Hemphill, you need to do your part, also. Rest, eat and no excitement. I'll check back in a few days."

Patrick squeezed Laura's hand and led the doctor into the living room. The doctor sat down on a chair and wrote a prescription for a sedative and said, "Give her one pill at night. This sedative will help her sleep."

"I can't stay with her during the day. I want to hire a nurse for her. Will you give me a reference?" Patrick said.

"That service gets mighty expensive, and they ask for money in advance."

"Money is no object. I want Laura better so she can work on our wedding plans," Patrick said.

"This service has an excellent staff of contract nurses," he handed Patrick a note with the information. "I know you'll be satisfied with their service."

"Thanks, Dr. Lynn."

Patrick turned back to the bedroom door and said, "Laura, I'm going to call Mr. Jacobs on the manager's telephone, and I'll be back in a jiffy."

"I'll be here when you get back," she croaked, trying to make a joke.

At the apartment manager's office, he made the call to Mr. Jacobs who said to tell Laura to get well soon.

After a couple of phone calls, Patrick had hired a private nurse to stay with Laura twelve hours a day and more if needed. After he explained the situation to the apartment manager, he asked, "Do I have your permission to install a telephone in my apartment."

"It'll save you from running up and down to use mine. Sure. I'll call Memphis Telephone to have it installed."

Patrick tore a check out of his checkbook, signed it and gave it to the manager. "Here's a blank check for the telephone. Just tell me the amount you wrote it for."

"Thanks, Mr. McBride."

"That's for the telephone company."

"Thanks for trusting me."

Miss Bradshaw, from the nursing service, arrived at two thirty-five. He paid her in cash, and she agreed to stay until he came home. He introduced Nurse Bradshaw to Laura. "Sweetheart, I hired Nurse Bradshaw to stay with you during the day. She'll get you anything you want."

"Does she cost a lot of money?"

"Not where you're concerned. Never worry about money. I have to go to work now," Patrick said and kissed her forehead. He felt the heat from the flu. He wrote down telephone numbers for Bonner, Sergeant Flaherty and Sergeant Roberts. He told the nurse to get in touch with any of the men in case of an emergency. Call Jacobs Department Store and speak to Mr. Jacobs if you can't get these men.

He decided to stay until the manager came with telephone installers. They arrived at four-fifty that afternoon.

Lieutenant Byers saw Patrick was not present at roll call and asked Sergeant Roberts about his absence

"His girlfriend is sick, and he had to stay until the doctor got there."

"That's just another 'X' by his name. I'm sure Bonner will be glad to see him go."

Patrick checked in with the desk sergeant ten minutes after six that evening. Bonner was waiting for him at one of the desks shared by detectives.

"I got your note about your girlfriend. She okay?" Bonner asked.

"Doctor says she has a case of the flu. She's tired, sleeps a lot and has a fever."

"That is flu symptoms, alright."

"I don't mind admitting that I am afraid. Laura would never leave work or stop planning our wedding unless something was dreadfully wrong. She's a strong person. What are we working on?"

"If nothing goes on tonight. Maybe we can sneak you out early."

March 10 1924
Dear Folks,

My Laura caught the flu. It is still around, the doctor said. She runs a high fever and sleeps a lot. We may have to postpone our wedding until she gets better. Will write more later.

Yours,

CHAPTER 24

GOOD NEWS, BAD NEWS

Patrick's mind wasn't on solving crimes, and Bonner appreciated his concern for his intended bride. He told Patrick to worry only about Laura. He had operated alone for a long time, and it didn't bother him, except for reports. Patrick had to come in and type them.

Laura stayed in bed for three and a half weeks, then she sat up and began eating solid foods. She had lost weight, and Nurse Bradshaw was determined to "fatten her up." Patrick could care for her at night, so the nurse's regular twelve-hour shift coincided with his schedule.

He told Bonner and Roberts the news and called Mr. Jacobs. "Laura is awake and eating solid foods. She's weak, but now, I know everything will be fine. She not contagious and can have visitors."

"Tell her not to worry about her job or being paid. She will get paid if she is here or not."

"That's a mighty fine gesture, but she doesn't need money. I've saved enough to take care of everything."

"I insist," Mr. Jacobs said.

I told Laura what Mr. Jacobs had said about keeping her job. She sighed in relief.

"My darling, I hope you can put up with me when the nurse is not on duty."

"I plan to put up with you for a long, long time, so a couple of hours will not make a difference."

Laura said. "How long will you stay with me tonight?"

"All night. We can talk about our wedding plans until you get too tired."

"Patrick, I'm afraid we'll have to postpone our wedding. I think I'm too weak to plan it."

"I'm not marrying a weak woman, so there. Just get your strength back, then we'll have the biggest, best wedding and honeymoon that these parts have ever seen."

"Thank you, my love."

Dr. Lynn came the next day. After examining Laura, he pronounced her flu-free. Weak maybe, but said he expected weakness after what she had suffered. Another week or so, she would be back on her feet and ready to go. Nurse Bradshaw stayed with Laura while Patrick showed up for work.

Mention something personal in a police station and within minutes the entire judicial system knows, Patrick thought. Almost every Memphis patrolman and detective asked about Laura and hoped she would be up and about soon.

"How are you holding up. McBride?" Sergeant Flaherty asked.

"A little tired, but okay."

"Don't overdo it. You'll make yourself sick," Chief Roberts said.

"I need about a week off to stay with Laura. Is there any way I can take leave without pay?" he asked.

"I don't see why not. I'll ask personnel."

Chief Roberts called Patrick the next morning and said that personnel had approved time off without pay. All he needed do was to sign the leave papers. Before Patrick could call Nurse Bradshaw, there was a knock at the door.

"Well, I wish I were a privileged policeman, so I didn't have to work," Albert Sidney said. "I got your leave papers, and Sergeant Flaherty said not to come back until you signed them."

"Come in, Patrolmen are welcome too."

Laura sat on the sofa and said in a loud voice, "Is that Albert Sidney, my favorite policeman?"

"It is I, prettiest girl in Memphis."

"When did I get promoted? You said your girl was prettiest in Memphis."

"That's when I had a girl. I don't have her, and she's not pretty.

So, you are now, by the authority invested in me by Foot Patrol High Archival Society of Memphis," he waved his hands in the air, "declare Miss Laura Hemphill, soon to be ex-Miss Hemphill, the prettiest girl in Memphis."

Laura laughed. Something she had not done in a month. "Albert Sidney, you are crazier than my future husband."

He leaned over and kissed her on the cheek and said, "Patrick McBride, you are one lucky man. Goodbye, beautiful woman."

Patrick winked at him when he handed the signed papers to the patrolman and said, "You do have a way with words. When you're not standing on the ramparts protecting our city, come back anytime. Tell Sergeant Flaherty, thanks. And thank you. I'll be seeing you."

They came. So many that Patrick could not keep up with the names. Laura knew them all, but she tired quickly. He called Nurse Bradshaw to help and set visiting hours. The visitors list included: Laura's family; Judge and Mrs. Webster; DA Robert Ingraham; Sergeant Flaherty; Chief Roberts; Bill Bonner; others from Memphis Police Department; the clerks from Mr. Jacobs Department Store; and many Patrick couldn't name. Most came for Laura, but members of the police department showed up for Patrick. Now, he understood why cops always put up a blue shield for their fellow officers.

Patrick had two more days left of his week off. He didn't want to leave Laura, and he contemplated quitting the force to be with her.

"Laura, I have to go back to work next Monday. I don't want to leave you, but I feel it's my duty. If you tell me you don't want me to go, I'll quit tomorrow."

"Why would you do that?"

"Because I love you more and more."

"Patrick, you belong to the police force, and I will share a part of you. Just a small part."

"Okay."

Next morning, he called Laura for breakfast, but she didn't answer. He peeked into the bedroom, and she was asleep. She had a tiring week, and he let her rest. She came out of the bedroom at ten o'clock and had toast and coffee Patrick fixed for her.

"You look a little worn. Are you okay?" Patrick asked.

"I am tired. But I'm all right."

They talked about marriage and kissed and petted all day that Saturday. Laura laughed at his stupid stories about growing up in Kingsport and the adventures he had in Europe.

He didn't mention Beth Formstone. "We'll have a good breakfast in the morning. Nurse Bradshaw is coming at seven o'clock.

At ten o'clock that night she said, "I'm tired, my darling. I'll get ready for bed." She paused, then said, "Patrick, I want you to sleep with me tonight. I feel that I'll, we'll, miss something if I don't hold your naked body next to me for this one night. I promise I will never again pull another "There's nothing wrong with a little nudity between friends" stunt. I did get you with it, didn't I?"

"Yes, in the final analysis, you did. If that is what you want, then I want it too."

They pulled their clothes off and slipped under the sheets. They came together and held each other and whispered loving words.

"Patrick, promise me that if something happens to me, you will find someone to take care of you and make you happy."

"You're the only one who could ever make me happy." But he thought of Beth Formstone and felt guilt for it.

"Please promise me. I won't sleep if you don't give me your solemn promise. Will you?"

"If I promise, will that make you happy?"

"Yes, it will."

"Then, I promise you that I will find someone who will take care of me and make me happy."

"I will rest easy knowing you will have someone like that."

Finally, Patrick said, "I love you, Laura Hemphill. Go to sleep knowing that."

"You go to sleep, knowing I love you as much as any woman ever loved a man," she said.

He held her close and went to sleep until seven the next morning. Sometime during the night, he had turned his back to Laura. Now, he wrapped his arms around her and she felt cold. "Lord, please don't let my sweetheart be dead. Please, God."

Patrick held her to keep her warm, and he heard Nurse Bradshaw call. "Mr. McBride, I'll have breakfast for Miss Hemphill and you shortly."

A few minutes later she knocked on the bedroom door and cracked it open. "Miss Hemphill, you want breakfast?"

"Get out. Don't you see, I'm keeping Laura warm? She's cold. I must keep her warm."

The nurse looked at Laura and saw she was dead.

"Mr. McBride, Miss Laura has passed on. Come out, and we'll take care of her."

Patrick opened the nightstand drawer and pulled out his spare pistol. "I said get out. Leave us alone. My darling is cold, and I have to keep her warm." he said and waved the gun.

The nurse went to the phone and called Sergeant Flaherty.

"Sergeant, this is Nurse Bradshaw. Mr. McBride told me to call you if there was an emergency. Miss Laura died last night, and he won't let me into the bedroom. He has a gun. Please, can you help?'

"I'll be there in five minutes."

Flaherty walked down to the detective squad room and whispered to Bonner about Patrick and Laura. Bonner told Chief Roberts where they were going. The nurse let them into the apartment and showed them to the bedroom.

"Patrick, this is Flaherty. You need to come out now. Let us take care of Laura."

"I said leave us alone. Laura is freezing, and I have to keep her warm."

"Hey, McBride. I'm coming in to see you. Is that okay?"

"Don't come in, Bonner. I'll shoot the first son of a bitch that tries keeping me from my Laura."

"Ah, hell." Bonner said. "You wouldn't shoot your partner. Hold your fire; I'm coming in."

"Bonner, don't be stupid. McBride is distraught, and he'll shoot you," said Flaherty

"So, neither McBride nor I have much to live for now. Maybe we think life is not worth living without the women we love." Bonner opened the door and walked in.

Patrick was in bed with Laura. He had his gun on the nightstand. Bonner pulled a chair up to the bedside.

"Listen to me, partner. Laura is gone, and there's nothing you or I can do about that. But we can remember and honor her for what she was, a wonderful woman who loved you and wouldn't want you to do this."

Bonner paused for a reaction. "You don't need that gun. Just put it back in the drawer."

Patrick put it back.

"Come on. Get dressed. You and I need to notify family and friends and make arrangements."

Patrick hugged Laura's body one last time and put on his pants. He sat on the side of the bed and began to sob uncontrollably. Bonner put his arms around him and said, "Let's go for some coffee, partner. Both of us can use a cup."

Bonner and Sergeant Flaherty saw to the arrangements for Laura's interment and graveside service. They laid Laura Hemphill to rest on Good Friday, March 30, 1924. Patrick McBride and a contingent of Memphis police stood at attention when Miss Laura Hemphill went to her final resting place in Elmwood Cemetery among senators, governors and other Memphis notables. Charles and Lydia came to comfort Patrick, who was among the few that didn't weep at the grave service. Laura's mother and aunt knew he cried himself out two days before. Patrick stood with Sergeant David Flaherty, Sergeant Bill Bonner and Patrolman Albert Sidney Smith; he waited for the closing of the grave. Patrick thought of Beth Formstone, one of few times since falling in love with Laura. At the back of the shadowy recesses of his mind, he kept Beth's memory alive and wished her happiness. But now, to honor Laura, the young policeman contracted a florist to put fresh flowers on Laura's grave daily for one year. He postponed erecting her grave marker. It had to be a design that honored the love they shared.

Chief Sam Roberts told Bonner he thought Patrick needed time off.

Bonner objected vehemently. "He needs to get back to work. Something to occupy his mind is best for him now."

CHAPTER 25

HUBERT JAKES

ubert Jakes knew something was wrong when he parked his red Overland in front of the house at 110 Mill Street. There were no curtains on the windows, and the shades weren't down. He hesitated but had to know what happened while he was in Shreveport. Before he started up the walk to the front door, a newsboy yelled at him.

"Hey, mister. They ain't nobody there no more. Cops closed that whorehouse last week. If you want some, you have ta find another whorehouse."

"Where are the girls?" Jakes asked.

"How would I know? In jail, I guess."

Jakes thought, *My money is old Mabel's safe. I'll have to find a way to get it.*

He got back in his car and sat thinking of his situation. He owed over $2000 in gambling debts to Ronny "Loose Change" Butts. He had to pay him something.

If old Mabel hadn't stolen it, he had enough money squirreled away to pay Ronny off. He watched Mabel put $4,000 in a small makeshift wall safe. Jakes had hesitated to carry that much money on his person. If the cops hadn't found it, he could get it. *Old "Dumbass" Detective Rush likes to talk. He will tell me if the cops found his stash.*

Jakes used the phone in the drugstore. "Is Detective Rush there?"

"Yeah. Hold on."

"This is Rush. Who's this?

"Hey, Dale. Hubert Jakes. How's it hanging?"

"Old Hubie Jakes," Rush said. "Where you been?"

"Shreveport. Do you know anything about vice raid on a Mill Street whorehouse?"

"Yeah. I think Wild Bill Bonner and McBride reported it to vice."

"Did they find any money in the house?

"If they did, I didn't hear about it. Was that your house?"

"No. I was sleeping there."

"An old hag, named Mabel, is still in lockup. You gonna go her bail?"

"Why should I? I paid her well for a bed-warmer and a bed. Thanks for the information," Jakes said and hung up.Mabel's girl Janie warmed his bed and kept him satisfied. He promised to take care of her if she were ever in trouble with the law. *I will miss her*, he thought.

He went up to the house and walked around to the back as if he were a prospective buyer. Jakes had no trouble forcing open the flimsy door. Inside he went into the bedroom. The vice cops had cut the mattress open and broke every stick of furniture except for the chest of drawers. They must have gotten tired of having fun because the drawers had been pulled out, emptied, and slammed to the floor, but the chest stood unmoved.

The cops were looking for money, thought Jakes.

He slid the chest of drawers away from the wall far enough to get to the small concealed door in the wall. Jakes breathed a sigh of relief when he pulled the box out of the wall safe and opened it. The box contained $2,200 in small bills.

That old bitch, Mabel, stole from me, he thought. *Nothing I can do about that now. A thousand ought to be enough to hold off Ronny until I can come up with the rest.* Jakes needed a drink and drove to the Red Lantern.

"What have you been up to, Jakes?" the bartender said when Jakes walked in.

"I need a shot of whiskey . . . the good stuff," he said.

The bartender reached under the bar and poured a shot of rye in a glass and set it in front of Jakes. "Boys in blue are looking for you," he said.

"What boys?"

"That Crazy McBride. He and this other cop, Bonner, is looking to kill you. If I were you, I'd get out of Memphis. McBride is crazy. He'll be the one that'll kill you, for sure."

"Thanks for the tip," Jakes said, drained the shot of whiskey and left the Red Lantern.

So, Crazy McBride is going to kill me, huh? Bonner put him up to killing me. That son of a bitch Bonner is gonna find out who he's dealing with. I'll get him first, then take care of McBride. Jakes kept a .38 revolver under the seat of his car and reached under the seat, brought out the pistol, and stuck it in the waistband of his pants. Jakes had never shot the revolver but kept it in case some young gangster tried to rob him. He drove the Overland across the river to Ronny's West Memphis gambling operation.

"That damn Bonner, I should have killed him long ago. I'll ask Ronny if he knows somebody that will whack the bastard for cheap."

THE CASINO

From the outside, the building that housed Ronny "Loose Change" Butts' gambling operation looked like an old warehouse, but inside was a sophisticated casino with table games, craps, and roulette plus a bank of nickel and quarter slot machines. Casino hours were noon to five in the morning. The guard on the door recognized Jakes when he got out of his car.

"Been away for a while, Jakes? Are you still laying bets on the wrong horse?" he said as he opened the door.

Jakes gave him a disgusted look and went inside. Ronny was standing in the middle of the room talking on a telephone.

"You'll come up with it. Get it from your wife. She's rich." Ronny listened to the loser on the other end, and when he saw Jakes, he motioned him over.

"One of the boys will be over there in the morning to collect. No, I've waited long enough. Get the money," he said and hung up the phone.

"You got the two grand, Jakes?"

"Not exactly. I scraped up a little more than a thousand. The cops are all over me since I got in town. As soon as I start my operation, I'll pay you the rest. You'll have to give me a little more time. Maybe a couple of weeks," Jakes said and handed Ronny an envelope. Ronny opened it and counted the money.

"Hubie, Hubie. I don't want to do anything rash, like busting your head, but I need my money."

"Come on, Ronny. I always paid my debts; you know that. I've got a plan to bring in some big money," Jakes lied.

"Okay. I may be getting soft, but because you've always paid in full, I'll give you two weeks. But you come up with the dough, or else."

"You won't regret it, I promise," Jakes said.

"You're right. One way or the other, I won't regret it," Ronny grinned.

"Look, Ronny. If I wanted to have somebody knocked off, where could I find a cannon? Cheap."

"I thought you didn't have any money?"

"I don't, but I'll get it the same time I get yours."

"Why don't you do it yourself?"

Jakes paused before he said, "I'm not that good of a shooter."

"You're chicken shit. Get my money," Ronny said and walked away.

I ought to shoot you between your beady eyes, Jakes thought and touched the revolver in his waistband. *But maybe I will do Bonner myself. It would be more satisfying to put a slug in the back of Bonner's head. Yeah.*

Driving back to Memphis, Jakes began to formulate a plan to assassinate Bonner. He had to become a shooter. Lawson Miller, a war veteran, will teach him how to shoot the .38. Then, he could assassinate Bonner. Hitting him in front of the police station was out. That was too dangerous. A better idea is to park outside the police building, wait for Bonner to come out, and follow him. Or lure Bonner into a dark alley and shoot him.

Jakes would park his Overland several blocks away because it would be too conspicuous near where he planned his ambush. Jakes was still imagining shooting Bonner in the back of the head. First, he had to pay Ronny or suffer the consequence of a beating by Ronny's goons.

The con man needed money. What old Mabel left him was not enough to live on or operate any money-making scheme. He couldn't do the poison-his-wife-for-insurance-money again. It was too risky in Memphis. He thought of the dead-letter scam. *That's how I can make enough money to pay old Ronny Butts and have some left before the cops get wise.* He had to have a place to stay and knew that apartment rent would take almost all money left by old Mabel. Driving into Memphis, he saw a for-rent sign in front of the Downing Apartments. Jakes turned around and drove back to the apartments.

JAKES, THE CON-MAN

His ability as a confidence man was Jakes' greatest asset. Jakes paid three months of rent in advance and settled in his furnished one-bedroom apartment. He opened the *Memphis News* to the obituaries and scanned the notices. He found the one that looked promising. Albert Summers, the sixty-year-old man, died yesterday, with the funeral the day after tomorrow. Address in a middle-class section of Memphis. With letter-size paper, envelopes and an ink pen Jakes wrote:

> Dear Al,
> I don't like to ask for a debt to be paid, but I need payment of the five hundred dollars you borrowed last year. My wife is sick and needs an operation, and I don't have enough money to pay all the medical expenses that this will entail. Please send a postal money order or check to this address: Box 126, 122 Union Street, Memphis, Tennessee.
> Yours truly,
> Bob Owens

He drove down to the main post office on Union Street, rented a P.O. Box, bought stamps and put one on the letter to Albert Summers and dropped the envelope into the mail chute.

Jakes walked out of the post office satisfied that in response to his letter, a check will arrive in P.O. Box 126 within three days. If not, he would move on to another dead letter from the obituary.

He parked his Overland. Walking to his apartment, he met a pretty girl and thought how much he would like to take her to bed.

"Well, hello, Miss. How are you today?" Jakes asked.

"Very well, thank you," she said.

"My name is Hubert Jakes in apartment nine. You must have moved in while I was out of town on business."

"Yes, I've been here two weeks. Good day, Mr. Jakes."

"I didn't catch your name?"

"Millicent Blanchard," she said and turned toward her apartment.

"I make it my business to know everyone in these apartments. Especially, pretty girls. Perhaps you'd let me treat you to dinner some night," Jakes said to her back.

Millicent turned and said, "I'm not interested in going out with old men. As old as you are, you should be ashamed. No, you may not treat me to dinner."

Jakes blanched and thought, *I'd like to knock her pretty teeth out.* Jakes watched her walk away. *I'll get you, bitch. You'll be sorry. I'll take care of you.*

Jakes sent Levi, an alcoholic war veteran, to check his mailbox every day, and the fourth day, the Levi brought an envelope with $500 check with a note from Mr. Summer's daughter.

Mr. Owens, I'm sad to tell you my dad passed away a week ago. I'm sorry he did not pay you before he passed on. Enclosed is your check.

It was made out to Bob Owens.

Jakes opened a checking account in Memphis Trust in Bob Owens name and deposited $450 gave Levi five dollars and kept forty-five dollars. Jakes took the first step in paying Ronny off before his enforcers came calling.

CHAPTER 29

CRAZY MCBRIDE EXPANDS REPUTATION

Chief of Detectives Roberts walked over to Bonner's desk and dropped a sheet of paper. "Somebody shot and killed Patrolman Frank Stevens ten minutes ago on 340 Union. Get up there and see if you can get the shooter," he ordered.

They drew a Model T from the motor pool and hurried to Union. One of the uniformed patrolmen said he was first on the scene and Stevens died before the ambulance arrived.

"Are witnesses still here?" Bonner asked.

"I tried to keep all of them, but only these six are left," the patrolman said and indicated a group standing against a storefront.

"You take those three, and I'll take the rest," Bonner said.

"My three told the same story with little variance," Patrick said later. "Officer Stevens stopped a fellow on the sidewalk and told him he was under arrest. The man pulled a pistol from his back pocket and shot him. He was medium height, five feet, eight inches, red hair, wearing a blue shirt and brown hat. All witnesses put his weight at one hundred forty to one hundred sixty pounds. One said he saw a tattoo on the forearm but couldn't describe it." Bonner and McBride compared notes, and witnesses agreed with few exceptions.

"If you wanted to make a fast getaway, what would you do?" Bonner asked.

"Go across the river to West Memphis by a freight train or small boat."

"Follow me around a little longer, and you'll be an ace detective," said Bonner with a snort. The detectives drove down to the docks and questioned five workers. None had seen anyone fitting the killer's description.

"You think he would chance the footbridge on the side of the railroad tracks?" Patrick asked.

"Too noticeable. I'd opt for the freight train. Hide in the rail yard until one leaves out or catch one going east. Let's get to the rail yard."

The detectives parked near a shack where railroad workers waited to go aboard a train for repairs or to oil some locomotive part. Bonner walked toward the shack door, Patrick followed and saw a glint of metal from inside.

"Bonner, get down," Patrick shouted and pulled his gun.

Simultaneously, a muzzle flash and loud pistol report came out of the dark shack. He sensed the bullet go past his ear and fired at the place where he had seen the flash. He heard a scream of pain and walked toward the sound.

"Stop, you fool," Bonner shouted. "He may be able to shoot again."

Patrick didn't heed the warning and kept walking. Another loud report came from inside the shack. Again, Patrick fired, and the bullet found a soft target. He stepped into the cabin and stopped to let his eyes adapt to the dark. The killer stilled clutched a .38 Smith and Weston revolver. Part of his skull had disappeared from the destruction of a .45 caliber bullet. He was dead.

"Damn it, McBride. Didn't you hear me say he could still be able to shoot?"

"Yeah. I heard you," Patrick answered.

"Why did you keep going?"

"I wanted to get him. You know something; I just don't care anymore."

After the questions and answers about what had gone on at the shack, and the ruling that it was a righteous kill, the detective squad room settled down.

"Bonner, what happened out there?" Chief Roberts asked.

"McBride is living up to the name I gave him the first week we partnered. Crazy McBride. I told all Red Lantern patrons that he was anxious to kill somebody that day, and he is crazy. Wait till this gets out on the street."

GOODBYE MARMON

Patrick seldom drove the Marmon now. It reminded him of Laura and their happiest days together. He tried to remember her excitement when he bought the Marmon and loving moments riding in the car. These pleasant memories couldn't wash his mind clean of her suffering in the last days. He blamed himself for not marrying her in December instead of being practical by waiting until April. It was August eighteenth, five months since Laura died, and he still dreamed of her and felt guilty when Beth began to slip into his dreams.

Now, he hated the Marmon and decided to sell it. He drove to the dealership on Union and was met by T. Earl, still wearing his car salesman outfit, yellow polka-dot bow tie, blue shirt and green suit.

"That's a good-looking car, want to sell it?" T. Earl asked.

"How much will you give me, T. Earl," Patrick asked.

"Well, let's see. Hmmm. How about two thousand and five hundred dollars? It's used, and they ain't much of a market for Marmons."

"In cash?"

"No. It'll have to be a check."

"Okay, two thousand and seven hundred paid by check," Patrick offered.

"If you bought the papers with you, it's a deal."

"Make the check out to Patrick McBride."

He caught the rail to Madison Avenue and walked across the street to the Memphis Bank and Trust. He developed the habit of walking close to buildings instead of the near the street in case someone had a mind to shoot him. Just as he approached the bank door, a person ran out and almost knocked him down. The thought it was a bank robbery entered his mind immediately. He grabbed and held the person that had body-slammed him.

"Turn me loose, sir," Millicent Blanchard said.

"I guess you weren't robbing the bank," Patrick said.

"No, I am not a bank robber. Turn me loose, now. Or I'll call the police."

Benson, the bank guard, appeared, "Anything wrong, detective?"

Patrick let the woman go and the papers she held scattered over the sidewalk. He picked up as many papers as he could get while the woman and bank guard picked up the rest. Patrick handed the documents to her and apologized. She took the loose sheets and walked away without uttering a word.

"Appreciative isn't she," Patrick said to the bank guard.

"Miss Blanchard is a nice lady, just a little flustered," Benson said. "You caught her on a bad day. Her principal pushes her around."

"Principal? Is she in business?"

"No. Miss Blanchard is a school teacher at St. Anthony's Elementary."

"I'd hate to be one of her students right now," Patrick said.

He deposited his $2,700. He saluted Benson when he left the bank and walked back to the Adams Street police headquarters.

Days off didn't mean much to him. He volunteered to stand duty for anyone who asked. Bonner washed his sorrow away with medicine for his poor arthritic fingers from Big Town Billiards drugstore. Patrick had "work" for his catharsis. Seeing him hanging around the detectives squad room, Chief Roberts ran him out. Patrick decided to visit Sergeant Flaherty at the patrolman's assembly room. He saw Albert Sidney talking to the sergeant.

"Good afternoon, gentlemen. And I say 'gentlemen' with some reluctance since I know you too well."

"Well, well, sergeant. Look who's here. Ole Crazy McBride. Have you shot any bad guys today, sport?"

"Someday, Albert Sidney, You will push Ole Crazy McBride over the top," Patrick said. "How are you, my friends?"

"Good," Sergeant Flaherty said and chuckled at the repartee between the two.

"Patrick, it's been about six months since Laura died, and I think the mourning period should be over. If she were here, she would tell you the same thing," Albert Sidney said.

"Five months, twenty-eight days, but who's counting? I've thought about doing what I set out to do . . . go to Texas. But it's better to be miserable here and closer to Laura, than out there without all my friends," Patrick said, then held up his index finger signifying one.

"That's a good decision," Sergeant Flaherty said.

"I agree. You're among all your friends in Memphis," Albert Sidney said and held up his index finger touching his thumb signifying a zero. "I have a proposition for you. Lily, the love of my life and the most beautiful girl in West Tennessee, has a sister coming in from East Jesus, Arkansas. We need a date for Eloise. She's a couple of years younger than Lily but has a great personality."

"How much younger in years?"

"Ten years."

"I'd be robbing the cradle; I think not," Patrick said.

"Lily is fifty-two. You won't be robbing the cradle," Albert Sidney said and laughed uncontrollably. "Eloise is twenty years old."

"Every blind date I've ever had ended in disaster. I'm a fool, okay. It's your treat, smart aleck. Give me details."

"We're going to Top Hat Friday night. Do you have a car? Don't worry. We can go in my T. Meet me at my apartment around six thirty. You want me to write that down for you, old man?"

"Make two copies, one for yourself. I'll see you Friday night," Patrick said.

McBride unlocked his apartment door and paused to think how lonely it is for him now. He thought of Beth and about returning to Shrewsbury. If he found her married, what could he do but say, "Good to see you, Goodbye?" He would like to know if she carried out Colonel Formstone's plan for the inheritance or if his niece and nephew had gotten the money.

MILLICENT BLANCHARD

Twenty-year-old Millicent Blanchard came from south Arkansas where Prior Blanchard, her father, owned a cotton plantation. Miss Angie, the colored maid, became a substitute mother to eleven-year-old Millicent when her mother died. Even before the death of her mother, Miss Angie was essential to Millicent. As a six-year-old, she followed her around, so the role came naturally for both. As Millicent developed into a lovely young woman, it became harder and harder for Miss Angie to keep up with her. She hadn't approved of some the boys who came courting.

One day, she told Mr. Blanchard, "Millicent is attracting too much attention from them plantation workers. She don't need to be hanging around here since she graduated from school. You need to find her something to do with her life outside this old place. If you don't, she's gonna stir up a heap of trouble."

Mr. Blanchard took Angie's advice to heart and began writing letters to various schools for young women. After two weeks, he got the positive response from the Myra Sharpe College and Finishing School for Young Ladies in Memphis. After supper that evening Mr. Blanchard sprung his plan on Millicent.

"Millicent, you don't need to be here without female companionship. There are no girls your age except some of the migrant workers. Since your mother died, you've had the run of the plantation, and the men notice how you've matured. Eventually, there'll be trouble," Mr. Blanchard paused. "The Kalb boy that's been running after you is just the first. Miss Angie is too old to keep you in check, and I don't have the time. So, I've decided to send you to the Myra Sharpe College and Finishing School for Girls in Memphis. Now, don't go crying and taking on, because my mind is made up."

"Papa, that's wonderful. I'd love to go to school in Memphis," Millicent said. She would never let her father know how bored she was living on a plantation.

"You would?"

"Of course. I know I need an education, and one of my high school friends goes to Myra Sharpe College."

"Good. We'll go to Memphis tomorrow morning and enroll you," Mr. Blanchard said.

Millicent settled down at Myra Sharpe College and found she loved everything about it. She studied much harder than she had in high school and let nothing deter her from learning, including young men. Her hard work paid off with a diploma and teaching certificate. St. Anthony's Grammar School, a private Anglican institution, needed a mathematics teacher and asked the president of Myra Sharpe for a recommendation. Millicent got the recommendation and the job.

She wanted to move out of the Lowenstein House, a rooming house for single working women, and live without a roommate. Finding a place was a challenge. Most apartment managers would not rent to a single female. After some disappointing arguments, she found the Downing Apartments, with a liberal policy where single women were concerned.

After her encounter with Hubert Jakes, Millicent became more aware of her surroundings when she went out. Although she couldn't catch him, she felt him looking at her when she went to work and watching her apartment when she was at home. She wished her boyfriend, Freddy, former right tackle for University of Tennessee football team, had not left for California. He could scare that old man out of the apartments. Millicent thought about complaining to the apartment supervisor but didn't want to be called paranoid. And maybe she was.

Millicent's father gave her a small .22 caliber pistol for protection when she left home but she hadn't thought about it for almost three years. She knew how to handle a gun but hadn't fired a pistol since she left home. Millicent dug around in her clothes closet and found the leather bag that held the gun.

There had to be other single girls living in the apartments. Grading, making lesson plans and tests, and lately saddled with the banking and alumnae relations jobs didn't leave her a lot of time to meet neighbors. A weekend get-acquainted party sponsored by the apartment manager would let her meet other girls. She needed to know someone besides sleazy Jakes. The thought of him made cold chills run through her.

CHAPTER 31

BEATRICE SETTLES DISPUTE

"You are an idiot, Banny. We need money, and with the nod of your head, our financial trouble would be over. But, no, Mr. Smart Guy had to exert his power and refuse a good deal. After almost two years, I'm tired of waiting." Beatrice Bandon said.

"Yeah, well you're the one that insisted we should get everything or nothing. We could have settled long ago for one hundred thousand each, but no you wanted it all," Banny said. "And Bledsoe quit. We'll hire another lawyer."

The grapevine had it that the Bandon siblings were unreasonable clients, and two respected solicitors dropped them from their client list. Beatrice and Banny tried in vain to hire another solicitor, but only hungry Ben Cumming agreed to take the case. Cumming said. "I will need ten thousand pounds in advance."

"We thought you took cases on a contingency basis," Beatrice said.

"Not so. If you think you can get a lawyer to work on contingency, be my guest."

"We have five thousand pounds left to spend. We will give you that amount, and you can have ten percent of what we get from Formstone's will," Banny said.

"I'll take your case for five thousand pounds up front and twenty percent of any settlement I get you," Cumming said.

"Agreed," said Beatrice.

"Yes," Banny said.

"I'll call Hawkins tomorrow and set up a meeting."

"You'll call him now," Banny said.

"Perhaps I've made a hasty decision. If I cannot do things my way, you are free to hire another lawyer," Cumming said.

"No, no, that won't be necessary. You do it your way, but we want to be at the meeting."

"I have no objection to that stipulation, but I ask that you say nothing until I say so."

"Right, we can live with that," Beatrice said.

After leaving Solicitor Cumming's office, Beatrice told Banny, "That slut and her lawyers are worn down. We can ask for more than the paltry two hundred thousand pounds and get it. I want the plantation in India. Or the clothing business in Hong Kong."

"Look who is the greedy one, now," said Banny. "Okay, I'll go along with the bluff for a short time,"

Cumming and Kelly agreed to meet in the Hawkins conference room at ten o'clock in the morning on Thursday.

"The Bandons have decided to come back to negotiate," Kelly told Beth.

"Why?"

"Perhaps they are tired of going back and forth or tired of hiring and firing lawyers," Kelly said. "I think they are running out of money. I would prefer to offer the greedy two nothing, but I'll not have a life until this situation stops. Offer them the same one hundred thousand pounds each as a starting point. I will give them no more than three hundred thousand pounds each. If the Bandons are short on funds, they'll take the first offer."

"But if they do not come around?"

"We go to court."

On Thursday morning, solicitors Kelly, Hawkins and Cumming sat at the conference table waiting for the Brandon siblings.

At ten o'clock, Kelly asked, "How long do we wait?"

"Maybe another ten minutes," Cumming answered.

Five minutes later Beatrice and Banny came rushing into the Conference room with the Hawkins clerk following.

"I'm sorry, Mr. Hawkins, they didn't wait for me to announce their entrance," the clerk said.

"Not to worry, Trimble. It's all right."

"Have you begun talking about our inheritance yet?" Beatrice asked.

"Did you not say you wanted to be present?" Cumming asked. "No, we have finished our tea, and were waiting for you two. We begin now."

Philip Kelly asked, "What amount of Beth Formstone's inheritance will satisfy your clients?"

"Let us not talk about money now. I will tell you why we think the nephew and niece should get a portion of what Colonel Formstone left Mrs. Formstone; They are blood relatives whereas Mrs. Formstone is his wife in name only."

"Stop there, Mr. Cumming. What is this 'in name only?' Mrs. Formstone can produce a marriage license and witness to the wedding if she must."

"Everyone in this room knows the old gentleman couldn't have consummated the marriage since he could not, shall we say, get it up," Cumming looked across the table and grinned at Kelly and Hawkins,

"That's a rather crude way of saying due to Mr. Formstone's health, he couldn't have intercourse with his wife. And I resent what you are saying because there is no proof that they didn't consummate the marriage. Unless you have a witness," Philip said.

"I have many witnesses that observed the lack of sexual interest the old boy exhibited. His doctor will testify that he was incapable of sexual intercourse."

"If we go to court and put Mrs. Formstone on the witness stand, the jurors will take one look at her and find the will unbreakable. And we're willing to go to court tomorrow." Hawkins said.

In their mind's eye, the Bandons pictured Beth showing her beauty in a sexy dress. Seeing her, no man in the courtroom would not believe that Colonel Formstone, age notwithstanding, had not consummated the marriage. Cumming had not seen Beth and knew Hawkins bluffcd.

"Good. The sight of a grieving widow wouldn't affect an impartial jury," said Cumming.

Beatrice Bandon who sat behind their lawyer touched his should and whispered in his ear.

"Can't you see Hawkins is bluffing," Cumming said to Beatrice. "There is no way a man his age could have intercourse with anyone."

"Speak for yourself, Mr. Cumming," the sixty-seven-year-old Hawkins said and grinned at the solicitor and his clients.

"We want to consult our solicitor in private. Do you have a place we might talk in private?" Beatrice asked.

"You may use the small office next door," Hawkins said. "When you go out the conference room door, turn left. You will see a door on the right side of the passage marked 'office.' It is small with a desk and two chairs, and it affords privacy. Should we wait?"

"We'll not take long.," Beatrice said.

The three marched out of the conference room and disappeared.

"They know the game is up and are ready to negotiate," Kelly said.

"I believe we have solved one of Beth Formstone's problems. I fear that what comes next will be almost as troublesome," said Hawkins and asked, "Shall we order tea?"

"Indeed," Kelly replied.

Before tea, Beatrice and Banny Bandon and Solicitor Cumming came into the conference room with a look of defeat and sat down in the same places they had left. Kelly and Hawkins said nothing and waited.

Cumming cleared his throat and said, "My clients have consented to accept the two hundred thousand pounds each you offered in your client's name. We—meaning you and I, Mr. Hawkins, will work out the details and prepare the paperwork."

"I'm sorry, old boy, I didn't offer you two hundred thousand pounds for each of your clients. That was an offer to Solicitor Salmon, but not to you. Now, we offer the original one hundred thousand pounds each. That's two hundred thousand pounds. Not a bad take for doing nothing but complain," Hawkins said.

"That's ridiculous," Banny screamed. "We won't take it. You live up to the two hundred thousand pounds each, or we walk."

"If that's what you want, we have nothing to discuss," said Hawkins.

"Banny, shut up and sit down," Beatrice commanded. "I believe it is a fair offer and I will take the one hundred thousand pounds. This situation has dragged on long enough."

"But what about—" Banny begin.

"I said 'shut up.' If you don't want to take the offer, go on with the fight," said Beatrice.

"You've no backbone, sister."

"And you have no brain. I need the money," Beatrice replied.

"We'll have the paperwork ready for signatures this afternoon," Hawkins said. "You may come in tomorrow morning at ten and sign the papers. As soon as the signatures are dry, I'll hand each of you a cheque for one hundred thousand pounds. We will file in Birmingham within two days," Hawkins told them. "Good day."

Kelly and Hawkins heard them argue about the money until their voices faded out.

"I'll go over to Shrewsbury Inn and tell Beth. She'll be relieved and may sleep well tonight," Kelly said.

After Kelly told Beth that the Bandons accepted the offer, he said, "as soon as the court approves the settlement, you could begin selling his assets and to fulfill his request."

Hearing this, Beth broke down and cried in relief. Kelly held her, and she felt safe in his arms.

CHAPTER 33

THE ANDERSON SISTERS

Millicent Blanchard woke late and rushed out her door to catch the next rail. Julie and Madeline Anderson stopped and watched her come out of her apartment.

"Hello," Millicent said.

"Hello," Madeline said.

"Hi, I'm Julie Anderson, and this is Madeline, my sister."

"I'm late for work. My name is Millicent Blanchard, and I just missed the rail."

"Where do you work?" Madeline asked.

"St. Anthony's School on Poplar Street."

"We're on our way to a recording studio in radio station WMC. Poplar isn't that far out our way. We will be happy to give you a ride."

Millicent looked for a car, but seeing none, she asked, "You have a car?"

"Goodness no. We can't drive," Julie said.

"We never wanted to learn. Always date boys who have a car, is our philosophy."

"The studio is sending a car to us because we don't know how to drive," Both girls giggled.

Millicent learned they were singers and worked at the Top Hat Club, a nightclub that catered to the city's elite. Their popularity had just begun to take off, and they were in demand in Memphis and surrounding areas.

"I've been here two weeks, and this is the first time I've seen you," Millicent said.

"We most of the time we sleep late, that's why you haven't seen us," Madeline said.

"It's a relief to know other unmarried women living here. There's a creepy man that keeps watching me, but it may be my imagination." Millicent said. "I'd love to hear you sing. Is there someplace I can see your performance?"

"We're appearing at Top Hat during the week unless our agent books in a special performance," Madeline said. "We'll be at the Butterfield Plantation for a private party, two weeks from now. Maybe we can get you an invitation from us. This week we're at the Top Hat all week."

"You'll need an escort," Julie said.

"The way things are, I'll have to order a date from Sears and Roebuck."

"Here's our car," Madeline said.

The Anderson sisters dropped Millicent at St. Anthony's.

"If you get a date, come to Top Hat Friday or Saturday night," Madeline said before the car pulled into traffic.

Lots of luck, Millicent, she told herself.

McBride Blind-Date Luck

On the taxi cab ride to Albert Sidney's apartment, Patrick pictured Eloise as about twenty-five pounds overweight and enclosed in a dull-colored tent-like dress. To make the image complete, he imaged she wore large white-frame glasses. The taxi stopped in front of the apartment, and Patrick sat without moving.

"Is this the right address, sir?"

"It is, but I'm not sure I want to stay. Let me think about it for a few moments."

"Take your time," the driver said.

Reluctantly, McBride pulled a five-dollar bill from his pocket and handed it to the driver. "Keep the change."

"Thanks, mister. Is it something you don't want to face in there?"

"Yeah. A blind date. Never had much luck on blind dates. I guess I'll make the best of it," Patrick said.

"Maybe your luck has changed," the taxi driver said and drove away.

Patrick slowly walked to the apartment door and stood. He knocked on the door. Albert Sidney opened it and said. "Come in, Detective McBride. Your date awaits you. I told her she would be disappointed, she insists on looking at you personally."

Patrick stepped into the apartment and looked around. He saw two girls staring at him. One stood about five feet, six inches; she wore her black hair bobbed, which complemented her dark onyx eyes that flashed mischievously. She wore a short gray skirt with fringes at the bottom, black net stockings with flat shoes. She was a real flapper. The other was shorter, dressed more conventionally, but also cute. He didn't doubt that the short one was Eloise, his date.

"Ladies, meet Patrick McBride. Memphis Police Department's own Sherlock Holmes. Also known as Crazy McBride."

"I'm Eloise, your date. And I'll say Albert Sidney lied about your looks. He said your face looked like a punch-drunk boxer with smashed nose and lips. Not at all. You . . . are . . . handsome."

"Hi, I'm Lilly. You're not crazy, are you?"

"Who cares," Eloise said.

"Come, children, let us proceed to my luxurious limousine, also known as a Ford Model T."

Albert Sidney's car allowed the two back seat passengers to sit with space between them. Patrick and Eloise settled in the back seat when Albert Sidney smoothly shifted gears and maneuvered on to the street. There was a September chill in the back seat of the Model T.

Eloise surprised Patrick when she slid across the seat and cuddled against him. At first, he thought it was an unintentional move, and he pulled away, but she got even closer forcing him to put his arm around her, and she put her head on his shoulder. It wasn't Laura or Beth, but he had a woman in his arms. The September full moon warmed his heart and made him feel better than he had for a long time. His mourning period started a long process of ending in the back seat of Albert Sidney's Model T.

HUBERT JAKES' OBSESSION

Hubert Jakes watched Millicent every morning when she left for work. He thought of ways to kidnap and rape her. He was obsessed with her calling him an old man. Old Hubie isn't too ancient to give her a bruise, and she'll live, but not long, to regret insulting him.

Planning revenge for Millicent's insult took Jakes' time and energy. He intended to write another collection letter, but he put off his next letter and concentrated on planning his revenge against Millicent Blanchard.

Mr. Knight, a professional burglar, made Jakes a duplicate key to Millicent Blanchard's apartment door. Jakes' obsession never let up, in fact, it had become stronger as he watched her leave for work every morning. Jakes used the key to search and sit in her apartment for hours. He looked at her family photos and began to bond to her image. He could take and leave women without a second thought. But Millicent was different. She would never have an old man which she made clear when he first saw her. The only way he could ever have her is to kidnap her and force her to make love to him. That wasn't rape. He didn't have what it took to use physical force. Before he realized it, two weeks passed.

A knock on his door roused him from his dream of what he would do about Millicent. He had forgotten about his promise to Ronny "Loose Change" Butts and didn't open the door. Another knock on his door and he shouted, "Who is it?"

"Leon. Let me in, Hubie."

"Go away. I don't know you."

"I work for Ronny. Let me in."

"Go tell Ronny, I'll pay him next week."

"Let me in, Hubie."

"Go to hell."

Leon kicked the apartment door in and knocked Jakes on his back to his living room floor. Ronny's collection agent didn't waste time. He pulled Jakes off the floor and cuffed him twice in the mouth.

"How much money you got?" Leon asked.

"None," Jakes mumbled through bleeding lips.

"Where's your money?"

"I told you, I don't have any money."

Leon hit him in the gut. Jakes fell to the floor and lay gasping for breath.

"This is a reminder that Ronny is impatient. He wants you to pay up, or next time I won't be so gentle," Leon said. He picked up a heavy lamp and slammed it into a glass coffee table which exploded, sending shards of glass throughout the room.

"Get the money," Leon said over his shoulder as he maneuvered through the shattered door.

CHAPTER 35

MILLICENT'S DATE

Millicent Blanchard wanted desperately to see the Anderson sisters' show at the Top Hat Club on Friday night. To get in, she had to have a male escort. Freddy, her boyfriend, left for California in May. Not having dated anyone else for almost two years, she was at a loss to find an escort by Friday night. Millicent asked her friend, Betty Jean, for help. She suggested Eugene Mansfield, a twice-divorced thirty-two-year-old. He was handsome with impeccable manners. Betty Jean volunteered to call him.

"He said he would be your escort if you paid," Betty Jean told her.

"I expected to pay something but not all," Millicent said. "But beggars can't be choosy. Does he have a car?"

"He does."

"I'll ask the Anderson sisters to make a reservation for me. Tell him to pick me up a six o'clock this Friday night," Millicent said.

Eugene Mansfield had two reasons to agree to escort Millicent Blanchard to Top Hat Friday night. She agreed to pay the ticket, and he could get into one of the nightclubs that had blackballed him. In a short six months after his inheritance disappeared, he ran tabs until club management discovered his financial status, flat broke. He still had his Bearcat and enough money to buy fuel. His friends furnished a place to live, food and pocket change. He didn't know how long he could mooch. He couldn't wait to see the bouncer Big Payne's face when he walked into Top Hat with this young broad who paid the tab. He didn't remember seeing Millicent but didn't care if she looked like a dried up old witch.

Mansfield, immaculately dressed and groomed, arrived promptly at six and knocked at Millicent's door. She had seen him at a distance, and his good looks up close surprised her. She surprised Eugene too . . . not bad for a little, old school teacher. A true gentleman, he took her arm and guided her to his yellow Stutz Bearcat. After settling her in the passenger seat, he offered her a scarf.

"Gets rather windy even with windows up. Advise you wear this, or the wind will blow your beautiful hair into a frizzle."

"Thank you," she said, and that was the extent of conversation until he killed the engine at Top Hat. He opened the passenger door and helped Millicent out of the Bearcat. They walked arm and arm to the Top Hat double door, guarded by Payne, the massive doorman. Before they got to the door, Payne bristled.

"Mansfield, I told you, you're not welcome here. Now get."

"I do believe we have a reservation in the name of Miss Millicent Blanchard, old boy. Check the reservation list, please."

Payne went down the list with his finger.

"Okay, Mansfield you go on in, but don't try to add to your tab."

"Not to worry. Miss Blanchard treats tonight."

Payne grimaced at what he heard.

"What was that all about?" Millicent asked.

"Nothing. A little dispute about overcharges."

The maître d' said, "Miss Blanchard. Your table is waiting. Follow me, please."

He led them to a stage front table and said, "The waiter will be with you shortly."

"Nice table. Must have cost you plenty," Eugene said.

"Not really. The Anderson sisters are friends."

The wine steward carried a bottle of red wine, placed on their table, opened it and said, "For you, ma'am. Would you like to approve?"

"No, thank you."

"I'll see if it's any good. A glass please," Eugene said. He took a bit in his mouth, swished it around, and said, "This does not meet with my approval. Bring your best and leave this one."

Millicent didn't object because she didn't know the difference between bad and good wine. Eugene drank a full glass, filled another, and finished it off. Before the waiter brought the second bottle, Eugene finished the first bottle. The restaurant had a limited menu, fish or pork with all the trimmings. The server asked if they were ready to be served.

"Yes, we are, and I'll have a dozen oysters," Eugene said.

"Sir, we are at capacity tonight and have a limited menu."

Eugene raised his voice. "Don't give me that, buster. Get me the oysters."

Millicent tried to make herself as small as possible and began to think she made a huge mistake. Eugene finished the second bottle of wine and called for oysters.

The manager moved Eugene's side and whispered, "Sir, if you don't quiet down, we'll ask you to leave."

"Okay. How about a bottle of Canadian whiskey?"

"We don't serve whiskey here, sir."

"I'll have another bottle of that wine," said Eugene louder than before.

"We have a two-bottle limit on wine, and you've had the limit."

Patrick, Eloise, Lily and Albert Sidney watched from two tables over. Eloise whispered, "I hope they throw him out. He's annoying."

"If you don't stop, I'm leaving," Millicent told him.

"You can't go anywhere without me, bitch."

Millicent left her chair and started to go. Mansfield grabbed her slung her down, and ripped her dress.

Patrick stood, hit Eugene, knocking him down. He reached down and helped Millicent up.

Eugene swung a wine bottle at the detective. Patrick countered and knocked Eugene down again. This time he broke Eugene's nose

"I'll have the police on you," Eugene screamed, holding a cloth napkin to his bleeding nose.

A waiter helped him up and whispered, "Don't you know who that is? It's that cop, Crazy McBride. He's killed four men already. You don't want to mess with him."

Patrick stood while Eugene looked at him and turned to go, but Big Payne picked him up by the belt and rushed him out of Top Hat. Millicent sat, clutching her torn dress top and crying with embarrassment. McBride took off his blazer and draped it over her shoulders.

"It's all over, miss. Don't be embarrassed by that idiot. Would you like to join us?" He pointed at Lily, Eloise and Albert Sidney, who was smirking with glee.

"No thank you. I want to go home."

"And where is that?" McBride asked.

"Downing Apartments. Do you know where that is?"

"Let me get you a ride home," Patrick said and walked back to his table.

"Albert Sidney, may I borrow your Model T for about forty minutes? This lady is distraught and wants to go home. That rich jerk ran out on her."

"Good riddance," said Eloise.

"Sure, but you'll miss the show," Albert Sidney said.

"You want to come with us, Eloise?"

"I'm sorry, Patrick. I leave for home tomorrow. I want to see the show if you don't mind."

"Not at all. Next time you're in town, we'll leave the wet blankets at home," Patrick said.

"Is that a promise?"

"You bet."

"Go ahead, McBride play the 'gallant.' I'll need my car back by twelve tonight."

"Come on, miss. I'll take you home in my friend's car," Patrick lifted her up and with his arms around her, helped her to get her coat from the hat check. Millicent still cried in the Model T.

Patrick started the engine and gave her his handkerchief. She stopped crying about halfway to her apartment. He walked her to the apartment door and waited until she opened it. Millicent turned and faced him.

"I cannot thank you enough, and I don't know your name."

"Patrick McBride. And you, miss?"

"I'm Millicent Blanchard. I believe I know you, or I heard your name."

"I doubt that unless you committed a crime. I'm a Memphis police detective, at your service, ma'am."

Millicent laughed, but she didn't know why. Patrick laughed too but didn't know why. Before she closed the door, he saw a small cozy living room.

Patrick missed part of the show, and the Anderson sisters came looking for Millicent at her empty table and asked why she left.

Patrick answered, "She's safe. I took her home after the idiot spoiled her evening."

"We heard about the commotion but didn't know it was Millicent until after the show," Madeline said.

At Lily's apartment, McBride and Albert Sidney said goodbye to Eloise and Lily. Eloise gave Patrick a very long and passionate kiss, finishing with, "That will hold you until next time."

Lily gave Albert Sidney a peck on the cheek. On the way to Patrick's apartment, Albert Sidney complained of Patrick's gallantry, and how Lily was pissed that he hadn't step in.

"That's the way to get killed," I told her. "And I want you to promise me you will never go on a double date with me ever again, Galahad."

CHAPTER 36

Lonely Sunday

Saturday night duty bored Patrick. He volunteered to stand Sunday duty for anyone, but no one took his offer. When you are alone and have nothing to do, Sunday is the loneliest night of the week. Patrick found himself in that lonely place. He canceled Sunday dinner with Emma and the judge, and regretted having done so.

Apart from Albert Sidney, his friends were married or engaged. Albert Sidney would be a pleasant dinner partner tonight. At these times, the Adams Street police station became his sanctuary. On his way to the station, on impulse, he entered Big Town Billiards and paused to get his eyes accustomed to the dark.

"What can I do for you," asked Frenchie.

"I want a sandwich in the back room."

"That room is restricted to good customers," Frenchie said and took a good look at Patrick. "I'll consider you a good customer if you don't shoot up the joint."

Patrick pulled his coat open to show he wasn't wearing his .45. He didn't show the gun in his ankle holster.

"Go in," Frenchie said.

He knocked on the door marked "private" and pushed it open. Bonner sat at the counter, nursing a whiskey.

"Hello, partner."

"McBride, have you given up your morality and come to the den of iniquity?"

"My morals are as strong as ever, but they let me have a beer occasionally. This is that day."

"Hey, Hi-Lo give this thirsty man a beer."

Hi-Lo drew a mug beer from spigot coming out of the wall. The froth spilled over and ran down the sides.

"No ice today," Hi-Lo said. "Drink it warm or not at all."

"I prefer warm beer," Patrick lied.

"What are you really doing here? Need help?" Bonner asked.

"I don't like to sit alone in my apartment, listening to the radio."

"My sentiments too. We in the same boat and mine is sinking."

"I want to patch mine, but easier said than done," Patrick said.

"You aren't responsible for Laura. My conscience bothers me because I am responsible for Sally."

"Let's go stuff our stomach at the Oak Room. I'm buying," Patrick said.

"I'm not dressed for your fancy eating joint."

"That hasn't stopped you going into your upscale places before. It will make us feel better."

"That was police business. Okay. If I'm asked to leave, don't say I didn't tell you so," said Bonner.

They entered the Oak Room. Bonner got a sour look from the maître d', but when he saw Patrick, he smiled and said, "Good Evening, Mr. McBride. I'll show you to your table. Follow me."

Bonner trailed Patrick who followed the maître d'. Bonner noticed the waiters were whispering and watching them.

After Bonner and McBride were seated and Bonner asked, "Are you a regular here?"

"I haven't been here since Laura died."

"Everyone knows you," Bonner said.

"Thanks to you and the name you gave me. Believe me, we'll get exceptional service."

Bonner laughed. Something he didn't often do. "Pays you back for the trick you pulled on me last Christmas. So, are we even?"

"We're even."

"May I take your order, Mr. McBride," the waiter asked.

"I missed a good Sunday dinner. Steak, medium well, and potatoes for me," Patrick said and remembered Laura with him at their first dinner with Emma and the judge.

"And you, sir?"

"The same. Make my steak medium rare."

"We'll have your order prepared immediately, Mr. McBride."

"Damn, you made out with the 'Crazy' name," Bonner said.

"Yeah, I heard I killed five men just for looking at me."

After their meal, dessert and coffee were served.

"McBride, you're a young man. A little younger than I. You should find a nice girl to marry. Or you'll dry up and become an old cynic like me."

"The night Laura died she made me promise to find someone to love and take care of me. That's hard to do. No one compares to her. I dream of her every night, not bad but good," Patrick said but didn't mention Beth, who had been invading his dreams.

"Don't you see. Laura gave you permission to let her go and be happy with someone else. When Sally died in my arms, she asked for help. I couldn't give her that. Killing Jakes is the closest thing I can do for her, now. My dreams of Sally are nightmares."

The busboys took the dishes away, and the partners had a second cup of real coffee.

"Are you going home now?" Bonner asked.

"No, I can't. I'll go to the station and look through cold case files until I get sleepy."

"This old man needs sleep. I'm going home. See you tomorrow."

After an hour, Patrick went home and went to bed.

"Patrick, my darling, this is a wonderful apartment, but not for a man. You need a place that is manlier. Something just for you and only you." Laura said.

Patrick woke up and looked around for Laura. Six o'clock. He had slept all night. He stretched to work the kinks out and thought of what Laura said in his dream.

Did she give him permission to move? If she had or not, the idea made sense. The Downing Apartments was his choice. Two Memphis policemen lived there, gave it good reports, and he had seen inside when he took Miss Blanchard home. Patrick called the residence management from work. After doing reports and paperwork all day, he caught the rail to the complex.

The manager showed him a one-bedroom apartment with

kitchen, living room and one bath. It was around the corner from Miss Blanchard's apartment. He rented it.

The movers came on Wednesday, and Patrick slept in a different place that night. In Patrick's dream, Laura kissed him. He woke up Thursday morning feeling different. She released him to live without her and find someone to make him happy.

CHAPTER 37

THE THANK-YOU NOTE

After the Top Hat date, Patrick decided that if he ever wanted to date girls without doubling with Albert Sidney, he needed an automobile. Patrick took the rail to Union and walked to T. Earl's dealership. T. Earl caught him as he stepped onto the lot. The car salesman changed his salesman's outfit to a pink shirt and yellow blazer. He retained his yellow polka-dot bowtie. A pink band ran around his gray hat. His shoes were black, and he wore white spats.

"Good day, sir. I see you are a man with discriminating tastes in motorcars. It's my specialty. Now, if you'll step over here, I'll show you one of the fastest sedans ever built. Gunpowder gray is my favorite color, and if I read you correctly, it's your favorite, also. This 1922 Marmon was driven to church by a little old lady for just a few months before great God took her to his mansions. You could say that this is a blessed car." He paused and put his hat over his heart. "I can let you have it for four thousand and five hundred dollars. Cheap at this price. How about it?"

"T. Earl, I owned that Marmon and sold it to you several months ago."

"You want to buy it back?"

"I want something simple but solid."

T. Earl thought about it with a hmmmm. "This 1923 Moon is simple, solid and fast with six cylinders, and its brand new."

"You sure it wasn't owned by a little old lady that drove it to church."

"No, sir. This motorcar is new and built for the road. You could drive this baby to California and back if you were a mind too," T. Earl said.

"You are one hell of a salesman, T. Earl. I'll take it," Patrick said.

"I didn't quote your price yet."

"How about one thousand and eight hundred dollars, cash? You drive a hard bargain."

"Let's fill out the papers," T. Earl said.

Patrick parked the Moon in his private parking space and picked up the mail, consisting of one letter and circulars. The envelope had no stamps, Miss Millicent Blanchard's return address. He opened it and read:

Dear Mr. McBride:

Thank you so very much for your kindness. I apologize for causing you to miss the Anderson sisters. Perhaps you'll let me make it up to you. The Andersons have wrangled an invitation to their next performance at a plantation party next Saturday night, October nineteen for one other person and me. Party begins at seven o'clock. I will be pleased if you consent to go with me.

Please let me know your decision by Monday next. I enclose my address.

Sincerely,

Millicent Blanchard

Patrick read the letter twice. He and Bonner were not on the duty roster for Saturday, October nineteen. His reply in the form of a note to Miss Blanchard accepted the invitation. He didn't know the location of the plantation or anything about it. According to Albert Sidney, the owners gave up growing crops years ago and rented the plantation facilities for weddings and large private parties. The location is ten miles north of Memphis on the high banks of Mississippi River. Patrick, with his reputation for being crazy, didn't want to go into a situation or party without knowing what he would get into. He called Emma Webster.

"Aunt Emma, do you know anything about a party at the

plantation next Saturday?”

“Patrick, it is mostly political. There will be one senator, two congressmen, all of the Memphis city council and two judges. Why do you ask?”

“A friend invited me, and I accepted. I want to know what I’m getting into.”

“Maybe Judge Webster and I will see you there. He is one of two judges invited.”

“Great. I’ll know three people there,” Patrick said.

“Are you coming for dinner this Sunday?”

After Laura died, McBride had a standing invite to Sunday dinner twice a month with the Websters. He enjoyed their company, and only duty kept him away. Mrs. Webster insisted Patrick call her Emma, but that was too informal, so they settled on Aunt Emma.

“I’ll be there, Aunt Emma.”

CHAPTER 38

Party at the Plantation

Millicent Blanchard called on Wednesday before the Saturday party.

"Hello, Mr. McBride. Millicent Blanchard here."

"Hello, Miss Blanchard," said Patrick and used the French pronunciation of her last name.

"Have there been any changes in your plans?"

"Absolutely not. I believe it will take about forty minutes to drive to the plantation, all dirt roads. I'll call for you at five o'clock if that meets with your approval."

"Oh, it does. I hope I can make up for that embarrassing incident at the Top Hat. I tried to get another invitation for your girlfriend, but the Anderson sisters couldn't swing it."

"She isn't my girlfriend, and she left for Arkansas after that night."

"I'm glad to hear that. I mean . . . well, you know what I mean."

"Yes," he answered, but he didn't know what she meant. "I hope your boyfriend is there; I like to take another couple of swings."

"He's not my boyfriend, and you knocked some sense into him already. You scared him so bad; no one has seen him since that night."

Patrick knocked on Millicent's door at five o'clock sharp. She opened the door. McBride stepped back and stifled a whistle. Her navy blue dress did nothing to hide her exquisite figure. Her short auburn hair framed her face and brought attention to her eyes, blue as a midwinter sky but as warm as spring.

"Miss Blanchard?"

"You have the right apartment, Detective McBride. I hope you don't make a habit of grabbing girls on the street, and if you do, make sure it's me."

"Ah, so you're the rude young woman who didn't accept my sincere apology. I needed no apology because that was the best part of my day. Maybe my week."

She rolled her eyes, "Now, you're flirting."

"It is getting a bit too serious here," Patrick said and offered her his arm.

The noise of the engine held their conversation to a minimum on the way to the plantation. The weather turned chilly, and fortunately, Patrick's Moon had an excellent heater. After he learned the idiosyncrasies of the transmission, engine, and brakes, he knew he made the right decision to buy it. Despite its name, it was a better automobile than the Marmon.

The drive to the plantation wound beneath overhanging branches of oaks. As darkness fell, Patrick noted the Moon's headlights were better than even that of a Cadillac's.

The Moon stopped under the portico. A valet opened Millicent's door and helped her out. The valet on Patrick's side opened his door. Patrick left the keys in the ignition and exchanged a dollar for his parking ticket.

"Thanks, Detective McBride. You scared the pants off old Mansfield," he said and winked.

Patrick gave him a half salute and recognized the waiter that helped the drunk at Top Hat. The couple made their way to the receptionist, and Millicent gave her the invitation.

"May I have your names, please?"

"Patrick McBride,"

"Millicent . . ."

"I need first names only . . . for name tags," she said and quickly wrote their names on name tags.

"Go in and have a nice time, Mr. and Mrs. McBride," she said, handing the name tags to them.

"A little early for marriage, don't you think," Patrick said and laughed when he pinned her name tag.

"I'm not engaged yet," she said pinning his name tag.

Arm and arm, they entered the great hall, which had been remodeled to accommodate large parties. On one side of the chamber, a stage had been set up for a band and singers. On the opposite side, men in formal wear crowded around a well-stocked bar with illegal alcohol. Waiters and waitresses scurried about, carrying food and drinks to tables. The couple chose a table close to the stage, where Patrick could observe the guests. He saw Judge and Emma Webster enter. Lawyers and even assistant prosecutors inundated the couple immediately.

"I want to say hello to Judge Webster and Aunt Emma. Come with me," Patrick said and extended his hand which she took. Emma Webster saw them wading through the crowd, waved and moved toward them.

"You know Judge Webster?" Millicent asked.

"Sure, old friends. If we can get to them, I'll introduce you."

Eventually, Patrick and Millicent met Emma Webster.

"Aunt Emma, this is Millicent Blanchard. Millicent, Aunt Emma."

"Patrick, she's lovely. Your description didn't do her justice."

"Aunt Emma—"

"Your nephew is so nice and such a gentleman. That's why I love him so much," Millicent looked at Patrick with mischievous eyes.

"Oh, here's Otis. Come, dear, meet Millicent Blanchard, Patrick's new love."

Judge Webster bowed to Millicent and said, "So nice to meet you."

"She's nothing like Patrick's description . . . much more beautiful," Emma said.

Judge Webster said to Emma, "I've warned you about the Cupid business."

"Oh, Otis, you're such an old fuddy-duddy."

"Patrick, come with me," Judge Webster said. "I want you to meet Senator Hill. A good man to know. Miss Blanchard, I'll borrow Patrick for just a minute and send him back good as new," .

Millicent winked at Patrick. "Don't be gone too long. I'll miss you terribly."

Judge Webster and Patrick walked toward a group of men standing near the punch bowls, marked "yes" and "no."

· · ·

"Isn't that just like men to leave their women to fend for themselves," Emma said. "Otis thinks the world of Patrick, and so do I. He's been unhappy for a while, and I don't want him to be hurt."

"Why is he unhappy. He hasn't told me anything."

"Laura Hemphill, the love of his life, died almost a year ago, Patrick hasn't let her go yet. Otis says he put himself in dangerous situations for that reason."

"He didn't tell me any of this," Millicent said.

"He keeps things bottled up. I keep hoping he will open up to someone."

"Okay, ladies, the Anderson sisters are about to entertain us. Let us find a table," the judge said.

"Millicent and I have reserved a table near the stage. I believe that waiter has it covered," Patrick said. He took Millicent's hand and led them to the reserved table.

"I didn't think you could reserve a table," Millicent whispered.

"There are mystical things police detectives can do."

She squeezed his hand.

Madeline and Julie Anderson lived up to their billing. The band began with an introductory tune, and the MC came to the microphone and said, "Ladies and gentlemen, we have a special treat. Please welcome the Memphis sweethearts, Julie and Madeline Anderson. Come on out, girls!"

The sisters came on stage and took their place at the microphone. The band began the intro, and the girls sang, "It Had to Be You" together. Julie sang "Some Body Loves Me" followed by Madeline's "I'll See You in My Dreams." The sisters sang "Hard Hearted Hanna." They performed "Big Bad Bill Is Sweet William Now," a comedy routine with the band.

The sisters finished their performance with "Roses of Picardy." Patrick's heart skipped a beat when the song reminded him of Beth and their time on the *Aquitania*. How could they have been so in love without telling each other how they felt. And how could she forget their promises. No one could take away his memories of their romance. He still thought of her as his rose and swore he would go back to Shrewsbury to find her.

The Anderson sisters came to Patrick's table and greeted Millicent. "Is this the guy you ordered from Sears and Roebuck?" Madeline asked.

"He's much better than anything in the Sears and Roebuck catalog," Julie said and rolled her eyes.

"Meet Patrick McBride," Millicent said and added, "A Memphis police detective. And this is Judge Otis Webster and Emma."

Patrick looked puzzled at the sisters' remarks.

"I'll explain later," Millicent told him.

After the Anderson sisters finished their part of the show, James Bell and his orchestra played popular songs for couples to dance. Patrick surprised Millicent with his dancing ability.

"Where did you learn to dance, Patrick? You're good."

"I spent five days on a ship and danced every night," he answered and thought of Beth.

After the last dance, the judge and Emma walked outside with Patrick and Millicent. The judge's black car appeared like magic. Patrick gave his ticket to the same young man who had parked it.

"Could we drop you somewhere?" asked the judge.

"Thanks, Judge. I again have a car."

"You *are* coming tomorrow for Sunday dinner, Patrick," Emma said.

"I'll crawl a mile for your wonderful potato salad, Aunt Emma."

"You'll bring Millicent, also?"

"We'll see what she has planned," he said.

The two couples said good night.

The valet stopped the Moon under the portico, gave Patrick the key and held the door open. Patrick passed him a substantial tip. An attendant opened the door for Millicent and closed the door after she had settled in.

An hour later Patrick parked the Moon in front of Millicent's apartment and walked her to the door.

"Would you like to come in for a coffee or tea?" she asked.

"I not sure that it's proper, I've known you only a short time. Tell me about the Sears and Roebuck comment."

"I once told the Andersons if I wanted a date, I had to order one from Sears and Roebuck."

"Well, did you?"

"I wish I had, after my experience with Eugene."

"I know what you mean. I'd like to get another crack at that old boy."

"Patrick, do you predict the future? Now, you tell me, how could I be the girl you described to Emma?"

"I haven't described any girl. You're the second girl I've dated in six months. As the judge said, Emma is always playing Cupid. She thinks I should go out more."

"I saw your reaction to 'Roses of Picardy.' What was that all about?"

"It's a long story for a future date."

"Emma invited me to dinner tomorrow. She's delightful, and I'd like to go."

Patrick looked at her in deep thought and finally said, "I like you, Millicent, and want to be friends. I'm not quite ready for anything else. Perhaps in time."

"I am in the same position. Being a friend is fine with me."

"Miss Blanchard, thanks for the invitation. You were and are beautiful," Patrick said.

From her apartment door, Millicent watched him walk toward his apartment thinking what a catch he would be.

CHAPTER 39

UNEXPECTED CALL

"Hello."

"Is this Patrick McBride?"

"Yes."

"Hi, Patrick. This is Millicent Blanchard,"

"Hi, I'm glad to hear from you. Gives me a break from the routine here."

"Will you have any time to have supper with me at the Meridian Café this week?"

"Yes. I can arrange it. When?"

"Tomorrow evening at six," Millicent said.

"I'll be there. Thanks," Patrick said and thought, *How strange, a call out of the blue*, But he didn't mind since he needed someone beside cops to listen to him.

"See you there."

He hung up the phone and looked around his pristine apartment. It was cold and lonely. His work caught up with him, and he felt drained. He had to sleep, but the dreams of Laura woke him up several times a night. Patrick checked his calendar. Tuesday, October twenty-second. From the deep recesses of his mind the image of Beth Formstone surfaced. Why couldn't she have been at her house? What comfort she could be during this empty time in his life. Next year his vacation time will be spent in Shrewsbury, England. If Beth were married it will make no difference, he longed to see her.

"Did you sleep last night?" Bonner asked.

"Better than usual. Mr. Weary came down and put me under."

"I don't tell a man what to do, God knows I made so many wrong decisions I've lost count. I hate someone to say, 'if I were you,' but I'll do it anyway. In your situation, you should move to another apartment. As long as you live there, Laura will stay with you."

"It will be a mighty long time before I won't think of her. I do have a date tonight."

"I tell you what you will do. You'll compare her to Laura. It is hard to do, but don't compare. Each woman is different. You can't put one beside another," Bonner said.

"Okay, Dad. I take your advice to heart."

"McBride, don't be such a smartass."

Millicent waited inside the Meridian Café door. Patrick saw her, opened the door, and held it for an old man.

"Thanks, sonny,

"You're welcome."

"Is that your wife?" the old man asked.

"No, sir," Patrick answered and walked to where Millicent waited.

"Marry her," he said loudly.

"You are lovely tonight, Miss Blanchard," Patrick said to Millicent. He remembered that Bonner said don't compare her to Laura, but he compared her to Beth. He knew it wasn't fair.

"You don't have to be formal. I'm Millicent, Patrick," she said with a pout.

"Very well. Let's sit at the corner table." He gently took her arm and guided her to the table. He pulled a chair out and invited her to sit. She looked at him.

"My dates usually put me in the back," she said.

"I have to face the door. A habit I developed."

"Like the walking close-to-a-building habit?

"Yes. Never eaten here, what do you recommend?"

"The T-bone is good. I prefer their fried chicken on Sunday."

The waitress appeared and asked for their order. Both ordered steak with trimmings and sweet ice tea.

"What have you been up to, Millicent? Dated any swells lately?"

"You are evil, Patrick McBride. No, I have not. I waited for you to call."

"I didn't know you had a phone."

"Installed a week ago."

"How could I have your number when I didn't know you had a phone."

"Touché. Here's my number. Now call me."

"I thought you had supper with your friends on Wednesday night."

"You are wrong as usual. Once a week we have supper together. This week I chose to go with another more interesting friend, namely you."

"I feel honored," he said. "Let's you and I start a weekly supper meeting. I'll miss one if I have duty."

She has a good sense of humor and pretty, too. Millicent will be a good friend, he thought.

"Fabulous. Do we meet every Wednesday?"

"Yes. That's settled. Now, what do we talk about? Certainly not that Mansfield character," Patrick said.

"I heard you are called Crazy McBride. Why?"

"My partner gave me that name, so some members of the dark side to remember and think twice before committing criminal acts."

"Does it work?"

"Your Mansfield scrambled for the door when the waiter told him my name."

"Why do you keep saying 'your Mansfield?' He cost me money, and I never want to see him again," said Millicent.

"Sorry. How did the swell cost you money?"

"He owns that Bearcat. Otherwise, he is flat broke. He agreed to escort me if I paid."

"That was a good deal . . . for him," Patrick said.

"Oh, let's change the subject. Have you been married?"

Patrick paused and finally said, "No. Almost, but no."

"If that's a sore subject, I'll not mention it again."

"It's too early for me to tell you. Maybe someday I will," Patrick said.

After their steak supper, they talked about growing up and how they got to Memphis.

He told her the story about rescuing Emma Webster.

Patrick paid the ticket, and the two walked down the street window shopping.

"I guess it's time for you to get home," Patrick said.

"Yes, but I'm enjoying the company."

"So am I. This is therapy for me."

"When do you go to work?"

"As soon as I take you home," Patrick said.

"You're not sleeping in your apartment?"

"I sleep at the station. It's more convenient, and my apartment is a lonely place."

The conversation died in the car. Patrick escorted her to the apartment and waited until she unlocked the door.

"Won't you come in for a coffee?"

"The neighbors will gossip. Good night, Millicent. Thanks for a great time."

"Good night, Patrick," she said and wanted to kiss him, but refrained. He looked lonely walking to his car.

CHAPTER 40

SILVER DOLLAR SAM

Benny Kearns, arrested at the Red Lantern, came before the court and pleaded self-defense for killing his competition. The jury found him not guilty, and he was back in business before the month was out. By undercutting his competitors, he expanded his liquor distribution business, negotiated a truce with his only competitor, and divided the area around Memphis. Kearns claimed Memphis and a twenty-five-mile radius around the city. His competitor agreed on taking everything on the Arkansas side, west of Memphis plus all area outside perimeter. Distributing liquor was Kearns' only business. He didn't want to be involved in prostitution or gambling. He found were too high maintenance.

Every week in 1924, newspapers ran pictures of revenue agents or local sheriffs busting whiskey stills. Around Memphis, anyone could obtain alcohol within two miles of his or her house. Even the corner drugstore sold alcohol. As a liquor distributor, Benny Kearns never had trouble buying rotgut and white lighting. There were plenty of stills operating in Tennessee, Kentucky, and northern Mississippi. Premium whiskeys, Scotch, Canadian, rye, gin, rum and others made outside the USA, were expensive and harder to get. Scotch and Canadian whiskey and gin came through Al Capone's syndicate out of Chicago. Rye, rum, and tequila came from Cuba through the Matranga family in New Orleans.

Kearns bribed state and local government workers, who controlled prohibition enforcement, to look the other way. There were a few federal agents that could be bought, but in those cases, it was usually a bother or brother-in-law that act as a go-between. After Kearns' murder charge didn't stick, he had the Memphis liquor business to himself and expected no problems for as long as Prohibition lasted.

The Matranga family was the Black Hand Gang, in New Orleans, and had controlled all vice in the Crescent City for forty years. When the United States became the only Christian country in the world to ban alcoholic drinks, the Matranga family became one of the largest distributors of illegal whiskey south of Chicago. Silvestro Carollo, a high-ranking member of the New Orleans crime family, became head of the family with the retirement of Charles Matranga in 1922.

Known as Silver Dollar Sam, Carollo began to execute his plan to take over the alcohol distribution business as far as his organization could reach along the Gulf Coast. Silver Dollar Sam was ambitious, not stupid. He beat his competition without a strong arm, but by hijacking their trucks and selling their whiskey at lower prices with insured deliveries. His competitors couldn't complain to the law because they were engaged in illegal trade. Local authorities didn't care or were paid off by the Matranga family.

Carollo sent his representatives to an area or city to scout out the market. He wanted to know if there were enough customers to make his effort pay off, what the competitors' strengthes were like, and whether he could entice the market, gin joints, and speakeasies, to drop getting supplied by his competition and buy from his organization. He expanded the family business by taking over distribution from Galveston, Texas to Mobile, Alabama. Silver Dollar Sam always sent two seasoned salesmen to talk to customers about buying his whiskey without intimidation.

The Matranga Crime family pushed all but a few whiskey distributors out of business. They discovered it wasn't worth the effort to strangle the white liquor trade even if they had tried.

Sam's liquor sales went as far as Greenville, Mississippi and stopped there. The Matranga representatives found that the people preferred white whiskey or moonshine over the more sophisticated liquors.

Memphis, Tennessee, the next city up the Mississippi River, had a large market with enough nightclubs and speakeasies to make transporting and selling contraband profitable. Sam wanted to see if his operation could take that whiskey business from the present supplier. He chose Little Walter and Big Bruce to explore the market to discover how hard it would be to push other suppliers out of business and to determine whether it would it be profitable. Little Walter was smart, and Big Bruce was intimidating. This combination worked well in other large cities, and Memphis was no different.

The Matranga family boss instructed the pair to do nothing to call attention to themselves. "Keep a low profile and do not let the law know you're in town."

Big Bruce and Little Walter showed up in Memphis and checked into the Senator Lane Hotel, a railroad station hotel. The Senator Lane Hotel sat two blocks from Union Station. When it opened in 1893, the newspapers called it the most advanced hotel in Memphis. It had flush toilets, hot water, steam heat, and gas lights. The décor transported patrons to Arabia with expensive Turkish carpets and lush drapes. At first, hotel management wanted employees to dress and work in Aladdin costumes, but no one applied for hotel jobs. The owners were forced to give up their grandiose idea of costumes and settle for the traditional uniforms and formal dress. Diners ordered food most people in Memphis had never seen or eaten. After a couple of months, the restaurant manager changed the menu to a more local bill-of-fare. Travelers kept the occupation rate to 90 percent, phenomenal for high-priced rooms.

Over time the grandeur of the Senator Lane Hotel deteriorated to the point where even traveling salesmen refused to stay there. The army of servants, bellboys, and stiffly dressed clerks dwindled down to one man on the desk and one bellboy. Fried eggs and hamburgers turned an elegant hotel restaurant into a greasy spoon. A person could rent a room for an hour, a day or a week without questions asked. Their customers were transient, and if a person needed to be invisible, he or she booked a room and disappeared behind the sun-faded drapes. While the outside looked sad and inside décor ragged, surprisingly, management kept the rooms clean even if the furniture appeared to have gone through a war.

Big Bruce and Little Walter booked the presidential suite in Senator Lane without anyone seeing or caring about Bruce's appearance. Little Walter complained about the shabby drapes and worn furniture, but Bruce didn't notice for he had other things on his mind.

They begin visiting gin joints and speakeasies to feel out what the owners thought of their whiskey supplier. What they found wasn't favorable for a takeover. Kearns' customers liked him and his prices. The Matranga family would have to put more pressure on speakeasy owners than was worth the effort.

Big Bruce was itching for action. He left Little Walter at the hotel and cruised Memphis for a pimp to supply a girl. Bruce entered the Red Lantern, one of the gin joints, the two had visited that day. The owner had hinted he could provide entertainment. Bruce sat at the bar alone. The freight train left a few minutes before, and railroad workers were still at work.

"Hey, bartender, I'll have a sidecar," Bruce said.

"Listen, buddy. I don't have no cognac, and I don't make no sidecars."

"That's what I thought. If you come with Silver Dollar Sam, you could serve a sidecar. Okay, a southside."

"I told you guys, I don't want to change suppliers and that's that."

"I'm not here selling liquor. Do you know a pimp? I'm not going to some fancy whorehouse, understand?"

"Yeah," the bartender said. "But the only one I know is in jail. You don't need no pimp if you're not choosy. See that woman," he pointed to a woman at the end of the bar. "Go over and talk to her. Old Virginia may like you."

Big Bruce looked at the woman and decided he could not be picky and walked to where Old Virginia sat. "You want a whiskey?" he asked.

Virginia didn't wear fashionable clothes and didn't care how she appeared. The U. S. Army buried her husband somewhere in France, and her two children died in a house fire. Before she began to drink, Virginia had been a pretty woman, but whiskey aged her twenty years beyond her thirty-two years. Bruce was not interested in looks, conversation or companionship. He was intent on having sex. The bartender watched Bruce and Virginia leave.

"Where the hell have you been?" Little Walter asked before Big Bruce closed the hotel room door behind him.

"Having fun with a woman."

"Your face looks like it's been through a meat grinder. Did she give you the scratches on your face?"

"Yeah."

"Where did you get a woman?"

"Picked her up at the Red Lantern. Bought her drinks and then took her out to back seat of my car," Big Bruce said. "I knocked her around a bit. She should not have scratched my face."

"You're stupid, Bruce. The boss said to keep a low profile, and you go out and beat up a woman from a bar. What do you think the boss is going to say?"

"He'll never know. She ain't reporting me to the cops. And even if she did, who is gonna believe a lush? The boss will never know."

"You better hope he doesn't," Little Walter said.

"When are we going home?" Bruce said.

"We go to West Memphis tomorrow to scout a gambling operation. It could be worth our trip."

CHAPTER 41

OLD VIRGINIA CANNOT TALK

Walking his beat, Patrolman Al Johnson heard Old Virginia moaning. She crawled out of an alley and laid there, "Help!" she croaked. At first, he thought she was drunk and couldn't get up, but when he stooped to help her, he saw she had been beaten severely.

"Don't move," he told her. "I'm going for help."

He called the duty desk sergeant from the call box. "She's in bad shape and needs a doctor. Okay. I'll go back and wait for the detectives."

The desk sergeant called Bonner and Patrick, who had night duty. Then he called the hospital for an ambulance and doctor.

"Get down there right away," the desk sergeant said." Old Virginia may be able to tell you something."

"You going to wear your top coat? It's chilly for October." Patrick said.

"No, I'm not cold natured like you,"Bonner said.

An ambulance and a doctor arrived at Patrolman Johnson's location and began to check Old Virginia for any severe wounds. There were none. The ambulance attendants placed her into the ambulance and left as Bonner and Patrick drove up.

"What happened here?" Bonner asked.

Johnson addressed Patrick, "Somebody beat up Old Virginia and left her in the alley. Maybe to die. The doctor said she would live."

"Any ideas who may have done this?" Patrick asked.

"No. Old Virginia hung around the Red Lantern and begged

drinks from customers. She was harmless," he answered.

"Alcohol got her. She's not old. Maybe forty. She started drinking after her two kids burned to death in a house fire. Her husband didn't come back from France, and she had no one, so the bottle became her only companion. I want to find whoever did this," Bonner told Patrick.

"Let's talk to Red Lantern customers," Patrick said.

The bartender saw Patrick and Bonner come into the Red Lantern they paused for their eyes to get accustomed to the dark. Carrying a bar rag, he came from behind the bar. "I don't want no trouble, McBride. I'll help you, if I can."

"Somebody beat Old Virginia half to death and left her in an alley to die," Bonner said. "She hangs around here.

"Has she been in here tonight?" Patrick asked. "And if so, who left with her?"

"Yeah. Old Virginia left with this guy from New Orleans. A representative of Silver Dollar Sam. He bought her a drink and they left . . . maybe an hour or so ago."

"Does he have a name?" Bonner asked.

"Bruce. His partner called him 'Big Bruce.'"

"Do you know where he is staying?" Patrick said.

"One of the railroad hotels. I don't know which," the bartender said.

"If he comes in again, tell the beat cop," Patrick said.

"I will, Detective McBride."

Bonner and McBride walked out, and went to the Model T. Bonner drove away from the hospital,

"He is more cooperative now that he knows you as Crazy McBride."

"Thanks for the name, Bonner."

"Think nothing of it. Maybe Virginia can tell us something about this fellow," Bonner said and took the street to the Memphis Hospital.

The detectives met the doctor coming out of Virginia's room.

"How is she, Doc?"

"Broken arm and ribs. Her face is in bad shape with a shattered cheekbone, but Virginia will live."

"Is she conscious?"

"No. She's in a morphine sleep. She won't wake until tomorrow."

"We'll be back tomorrow. Maybe the old woman can tell us who did this," Bonner said.

Patrick looked in the hospital room at Virginia lying in bed with bandages over most of her upper body and thought of Beth. If somebody did this to Beth, there would be no hesitation. He would kill the man on the spot.

Patrick and Bonner sat in the Model T outside the hospital with Patrick behind the wheel.

"What now? Where do we go from here?" Patrick asked. "Should we canvas the hotels or have a uniform do it."

"You know I work a case until it's solved or goes into the cold case file. Unless we get lucky, it will take us a couple of days to canvas the hotels. Let's sleep in the squad room and hit the hotels tomorrow."

LITTLE WALTER AND BIG BRUCE CROSS THE RIVER

After searching for an hour, Little Walter parked at what looked like a warehouse on the outside. They got out of the Buick and approached the guard at the entrance.

"I don't know you two. Are you looking for warehouse space?"

Big Bruce walked up and without warning kicked the guard between the legs. The guard fell and passed out from the pain. Big Bruce, followed by Little Walter, entered the casino and looked around.

Ronny "Loose Change"' Butts looked up from his counting table and watched Little Walter and Big Bruce come into the casino. The two marched up to Ronny who covered the money with a glass shield.

"You own this place?" Little Walter asked.

"Yeah. My name is Ronny Butts."

"I'm Walter, and this is Bruce."

What can I do for you gentlemen? Would you like a drink on the house?"

"Teach your bouncer manners. And you'd better get him a new set of balls, cause after what I did, he won't be able to use his old ones," Big Bruce said.

"He is told to keep strangers out. If he doesn't know you, he doesn't let you in," Ronny said.

"So, we got in any way," Bruce said.

"We're looking to buy or start up an operation like you have here," Walter said.

"This is not for sale."

"How about a partnership. You keep eighty percent of the profits," Walter said.

"I keep all of the profits now."

"You need protection from an upriver operator moving in on your territory. We'll make sure it doesn't happen. And with us, you won't have any trouble with the law. You don't have to answer now. We'll give you a week to think about it. A smart businessman such as yourself will know this is a good deal all around," Walter said.

"Yeah. We'll be back next week. Tell your man to let us in next time, or he'll get more than he can take," Bruce said. "You have any girls working here."

"Yeah. Not during the day. They serve drinks at night."

"Maybe I'll come back tonight for a look-see."

"They are off limits to anyone trying to get friendly. Women guests must have a male escort to come into my casino. No hanky-panky on this property."

"We'll do something about that when we become your partner," Big Bruce said.

Bonner was right. The New Orleans Matranga family had finally came to visit.

Ronny picked up the receiver and told the operator Memphis police station. "Sergeant Manners, may I help you."

"Yes. I want to speak with Detective Bonner."

CHAPTER 43

Big Bruce Goes Down for the Count

Patrick answered the phone and handed it to Bonner. "It's your call," he told Bonner.

He watched Bonner talking into the phone. "Yeah. I'd want that big boy. He beat up a harmless woman and left her for dead. I want him bad, but I cannot do much about your situation. It's out of our jurisdiction. If I find out where they're staying, we'll go after them. Okay, Ronny. Thanks. I hope I can get both here." Bonner hung up the receiver and turned to Patrick.

That was Ronny. The New Orleans goons visited him today. He said the big one, called Big Bruce, talked about satisfying his sexual appetite with an old broad last night and was looking for more in West Memphis. He's the one that beat up Old Virginia. We'll get him here before they leave to go back to New Orleans. I have a feeling the two opted for a cheap transit hotel instead of a fancy one. Saddle up, let's search the railroad hotels."

Bonner and Patrick parked the Model T police car and walked across the street to the Senator Lane Hotel, the most logical for New Orleans hoods that want privacy without having to pay. The desk clerk didn't look up reading a newspaper when the two detectives stopped in front of him. Bonner slammed his fist on the bell sitting on the counter and screamed, "Service!"

The clerk dropped the newspaper and jumped up to face them. "What can I do for you, gentlemen?"

Holding up his Memphis police badge, Bonner said, "I'm Detective Bonner, and this is Detective McBride. We want you to answer a few questions; then you can get back to the funny papers."

The clerk looked past Bonner at Patrick with wide eyes.

"We're looking for a couple of goons that may be staying here," Bonner said. "One is a galoot that goes by Big Bruce. The other is a small fellow. You have anyone staying here that fits that description?"

"I don't look at everyone that registers, so I can't say." The clerk kept his eyes on Patrick.

"I want him bad. I'm so frustrated I could kill somebody," Patrick said and gave the clerk an evil smile.

"Let me think. Maybe I have seen the big one. There were two men registered here a couple of weeks ago. One was massive with a boxer's nose. The other was small and registered. His name was Walter Pier. I don't know anything about the other one."

"What is their room number?'

"They have the presidential suite on the top floor."

"Are they in now?" Bonner asked.

"No. The two left early this morning but are paid up for four more nights."

Bonner laid his card with the station phone number printed on it. "Call and ask for me, if these goons come back."

"Bonner, I have itchy fingers. I'm anxious to meet them."

Bonner turned and said, "Hold your horses, McBride. You'll get a chance, but no shotgun. Much too messy."

"Ah, Bonner, you're no fun."

The detectives didn't see the blood drain out of the clerk's face while he held onto the counter.

"We'll wait in the reading area for a while," Bonner told him and lit a Home Run.

Patrick sat in an easy-chair across the room from Bonner. Both picked a newspaper and began to read. Almost an hour later, two men—one large, one small—came into the lobby. Bonner pinched the fire out of the fourth Home Run. Patrick quietly put his newspaper down.

The two detectives stood up. Patrick pulled his coat aside and put his hand on the butt of his pistol. Bonner followed suit. Big Bruce and Little Walter didn't pay attention to the two men walking toward them until the detectives were ten feet away. The hotel clerk ducked behind the counter.

"What the hell do you want?" Bruce said.

"You're under arrest for assault and battery and attempted murder. Stick out your hands," Bonner said with open handcuffs in his hand.

Bruce looked at Bonner and Patrick with surprise. "Like hell, I will," Bruce said and with a scream charged Bonner.

Patrick stepped between the two men with his gun drawn. Bruce tried to push him away to get to Bonner. He realized his mistake too late to ward off Patrick, who hit Bruce's throat with his gun. Bruce dropped to the floor and tried to breathe with loud wheezing. Bonner snapped the handcuffs on him.

"Hey, dumb ass, call an ambulance for this jerk before he dies," Bonner said to the clerk.

Little Walter did not move. Patrick said, "Walter, we aren't after you. We don't have anything on you. You are free to go or stay."

Walter watched Bruce struggle for breath.

"It's a good thing Crazy McBride decided not to use his .45 or old Bruce would be oozing life."

It took two ambulance attendants to put Big Bruce on a gurney and wheel him out of the hotel into an ambulance. Bonner and Patrick followed and made one stop at a call box to ask for a uniform to guard Bruce in the hospital.

Patrick entered the emergency room and saw two doctors working on Bruce.

"How did this happen?" the first one asked.

"I understand he tried to get away from a cop. He'll never have a normal voice," the second one said. "Why do cops do this to people?"

"I can answer that," Patrick said.

"Who are you?" the first doctor asked.

"Detective McBride. Did you see a woman, Virginia, come in a couple of nights ago? "

"Yeah." the second doctor asked

"Big Bruce almost beat her to death. Does that answer your question?"

"You said your name is McBride?" the first doctor asked

"Yes."

"You have a reputation of being a non-nonsense policeman," the first doctor said. "This man is lucky to be alive."

Bonner walked in followed by a uniformed policeman.

"Handcuff him to the bed and don't let him get up. If he does, hit him with your billie club," Bonner told the policeman.

"Are you ready to go?" Patrick asked Bonner.

"Let's go."

In the detective squad room, Patrick told Bonner, "You write the report, and I'll type it. This one will be a pleasure."

"Okay. When you finish, we'll get a steak or something at the Meridian."

Patrick looked surprised.

"Okay, Okay. I'll buy."

"Bonner, you're not a bad sort after all," Patrick said and laughed.

CHAPTER 44

WEDNESDAYS WITH MILLICENT

Wednesdays became Patrick's favorite day of the week. He met Millicent for dinner and talked. Patrick thought of her a good friend in whom he could confide.

She listened to stories about growing up in Kingsport and his three years at Princeton. He hadn't attended the drunken frat parties. He didn't drink. Putting a cow in the president's office, by a group of students led by Patrick was the only thing he did. Member of the faculty asked him why he did it and Patrick said, "Just for the fun of it."

One night he told her about the song, "Roses of Picardy" and Beth. How his heart was broken when she had not waited for him.

"We knew each other for five days," he said, "and I fell for her 'hook line and sinker.' I still love her and dream of her often. It is strange. I feel she's looking for me. If she appeared here at this very minute, I would ask her to marry me. Next year I'll go back to Shrewsbury."

"And if she's married?" Millicent asked.

"I'll tell her husband what a lucky man he is and try to take her away from him."

"You love her that much?"

"I do."

"I guess that's no chance for me," Millicent said.

"We've been over this before. I can only say you are a beautiful girl and had I met you two years ago, this situation would be different. Today, I want to keep our relationship like a brother and sister. I love being with you. You're fun and easy to talk with. I can tell you my darkest secrets and know it will never be revealed to anyone."

"Speaking of deep, dark secrets, let's go to the theater and see "*Secrets*."

"That is a good suggestion. When?"

"Friday night?"

"Good. I need some good risqué entertainment."

"I think it is a serious film about what happens when a husband cheats on his wife," she said.

"I get embarrassed if it's filled with sex. I'll look at the duty roster and tell you if I'm available. I can't go after seven o'clock," Patrick said.

"Why?'

"I'm scared of the dark."

Millicent crumbled up a paper napkin and threw it at him, and said, "How could your two women love you?"

"I've tried to figure that out. I'm baffled. Albert Sidney said it would be my charisma if I had any."

"Smart man."

Patrick got up from the table and paid the check. Millicent followed.

"I have a hard day of detecting tomorrow and need my sleep. I'm glad we live in the same apartment complex. Or you'd have to walk home," Patrick said.

Millicent hit his arm and said, "Now, I know why I love you."

Patrick became serious. "You know I have to go. If I don't find out, one way or the other, I'll never love another woman."

"I'm sorry I said that. Please forgive me."

"You are a dear and are forgiven already."

Patrick waited until Millicent was inside her apartment. He didn't see anyone but felt someone watching. Had he known that Hubert Jakes lived in one of the apartments, the con man would be working his scams on a chain gang at the Shelby County prison farm.

CHAPTER 45

BETH'S SEARCH FOR PATRICK

I t took three weeks for Beatrice and Banny Bandon to rescind their caveat and receive their settlement after the court released Colonel Formstone's bank account. The fact that Beth had to give the Bandons a hundred thousand dollars each bothered her, but she had to do it to keep from stretching the process out to another year or more. The Bandons asked Solicitor Philip Kelly if they could meet with Beth. She chose not to see them for fear what she might say to them after what they had called her.

"To fulfill the colonel's wishes will be another long and tedious job." Kelly told her. "We have to list his assets before selling them. You have completed most of the list. And then, we make sure all his debts are found and paid, if any, before beginning to meet the stipulations of his will. We have to report all actions to the court to satisfy the court that you, as his heir, will carry out his wishes to give money to his charities and not abscond with the funds. Once we sell his assets, we pay estates taxes to the Revenue Department."

The next day the two took a train to Birmingham. The court magistrate advised them to report the sale of the colonel's assets weekly.

"Colonel Formstone left us instructions to transfer ownership of his one-thousand-acre cotton plantation to the people that worked the fields. Each of twenty-one farm workers receives a tax-free deed to approximately forty-seven acres which makes an Indian farmer very rich. Farm the land or sell the land? The colonel, didn't specify. His British plantation manager gets his forty-seven acres and twenty thousand pounds for his twenty years of hard work and loyalty. Let's sort out the plantation first," Beth told the lawyers. "What they do with the newfound riches is their business.

"Our associate in New Delhi will handle the plantation transfer," Philip said. "Other assets will not be so easy. If we didn't have to turn every holding into cash, we could coast along. But with his request for cash gifts to be handed out, we have to buck up and take our time to get everything right."

"Mr. Hawkins is the co-executor, can he handle this phase?" Beth asked.

"Yes. We've discussed that action already. Ralph will relieve you of this burden. You will have sign off on his decisions."

"This is what I've waited to hear. I will begin my search for Patrick McBride immediately," Beth said.

With her solicitors Ralph Hawkins and Philip Kelly taking over the responsibility of selling Colonel Formstone's assets and distributing the equity, freed Beth to pursue the quest for Patrick. As co-executors, Hawkins paid her inheritance of five hundred thousand pounds which set her free search for Patrick.

She made a list of what she knew about Patrick McBride:

Home? Tennessee.
Father? the attorney.
School? He attended Princeton University in the state of New Jersey, studied law.
He loved history.

She didn't remember his hometown or where in Tennessee he resided.

I'll start at the Britannia Adelphi, she thought. The next day she exited the train depot and walked to the Adelphi.

At the hotel she asked the registration clerk how long the hotel kept guest records.

"Three years," he said.

"Good. I want the address of Mr. Patrick McBride from the United States. He stayed here in October 1922. I think, on the twenty-first or twenty-second."

"I'm very sorry, miss. Our policy is not to give out information concerning our guests."

"May I speak to the manager?"

"I am the manager. And we never break policy. I'm sorry we can't help you," he said.

Maybe Cunard has his address, she thought.

Cunard's office was practically empty. Only a shell from 1921 to what it is now. Cunard moved its office along with records from Liverpool to Southampton. Beth learned even if they could find his address, they wouldn't divulge any passenger information.

An agent said, "He may have booked passage on a freighter. You should ask the harbor master if there were any ships that left October 22 with a U.S. destination."

She walked to the harbor masters' shack and knocked on the door.

"Come in," a voice came from inside.

She quickly told her situation and asked the harbor master what ships left Liverpool on October 22, 1922. He pulled the file and scanned down to October.

"Ye say 1922? What date did you want?" He asked.

"October twenty-second," she answered.

"I had three freighters leaving on that day. One to Italy, one to India and one to the United States, the old *Bristol Star*. Captain Bob Jenkins commands her. If you can find him, he will help."

"Where in the United States did *Bristol Star* dock?"

"Savannah, Georgia. It's in the state of Georgia between Charleston, South Carolina and Jacksonville, Florida. Old Jenkins retired and lives in the country where I do not know. I'm curious. Why do you want this information?"

"I'm trying to find an American man who may have left on that ship."

"He stole money from ye?"

"No. Patrick McBride stole my heart," Beth said.

The harbor master chuckled. "I be damn. Aye, to be looking for him at this late date, he must be an exceptional fellow. Good luck to you, Lass."

Now, she knew where he landed in the United St*ates. That's something.* She remembered his mentioning Tennessee as his home, not Georgia.

The American consul. Maybe she could find out how to get his address in America, she thought.

She waited nervously for an hour in the American consul's outer office. A nicely dressed gentleman came into the small room and said, "Miss Formstone?"

"Yes."

"I am sorry to have kept you waiting. I am secretary to Consul Weaver. You're British. May I ask what brings you to our consulate?"

"To inquire about an American who left Liverpool in October 1922. It's imperative that I find him. He comes from the state of Tennessee."

"Perhaps we can help. First, what is his name?

"Patrick McBride."

"His address in Tennessee?"

"I don't have an address. I hoped you'd furnish Mr. McBride's address," Beth said.

"I sorry, Miss Formstone. With only a name and a state, we can't help you," the secretary said.

The door to consul's office opened, and Consul Weaver came out.

"Barnes, we need to destroy some of our papers before we leave. What do we have here?"

"Sir, this is Miss Beth Formstone. She came to ask our help in finding a Mr. Patrick McBride, an American," the secretary said.

"You go see about the papers, Barnes. I'll try to help Miss . . ."

"Formstone."

"Yes. I'll assist Miss Formstone," Consul Weaver said. "So, this fellow, McBride, is not a British citizen?"

"No. Patrick is an American from Tennessee. I want to find him as soon as possible," Beth said.

"Why? Did he take something from you?"

"Yes, he did," Beth said, thinking, *my love*.

"Miss Formstone, we are not an investigating agency. There are probably a hundred Patrick McBrides in Tennessee. Finding this particular McBride will take, entirely, too much time. Can you imagine interviewing each Patrick McBride? I'm sorry, Miss Formstone, I can suggest how to go about searching. I'll have Barnes prepare a list of Tennessee newspapers. You may have some luck by running notices asking readers for any information about McBride."

"Thank you, consul. I'll take the list."

American Consul Weaver walked back into his office, and Beth heard him say, "Barnes, get Miss Formstone a list of daily newspapers with addresses in Tennessee. Afterward come back and finish destroying the files."

A few minutes later, Barnes handed Beth a sheet of paper with the names of six daily newspapers. "I apologize for not taking more time. Our State Department insists we close this consulate and open a new one in Southampton by next Wednesday."

"Thank you for your time. Goodbye," Beth said and turned to walk out the door.

"Miss Formstone," Barnes said. Beth turned to face him. "What did McBride steal from you?"

"My heart, Mr. Barnes. My heart," she said.

Finding nothing to help her search in Liverpool, Beth took a train back to Shrewsbury. On the trip back, Beth begins to assess her quest. The odds of finding information through newspaper notices could take a year without results. If she went to America and searched for him in Tennessee, there would be no guarantee he would be there. He could be living in any state in the United States. He could be married or worse dead.

Maybe Philip is right about finding Patrick. It could take years, and the odds are too high.

What bothered her most was the fact she hadn't told him of her love. Beth concluded that they were like two ships passing in the night, ended the moment they left the RMS *Aquitania*. It was just a promise that they would not forget each other. Beth remembered how he held her in his arms and his warm, loving kisses, and she felt her heart skip a beat.

His note said he loved her, but I must get over this feeling of love for Patrick.

CHAPTER 46

BUSTING JANIE OUT OF PRISON

Hubert Jakes wanted to make one big score with Janie and get out of Memphis. A booming business climate in Memphis attracted conventions of professional associations from as far north as St. Louis, Missouri, as far west as Dallas, Texas and as far east as Washington D.C. He scanned the business section of the news every morning until he found the American Drug Manufacturers Association Convention, January 22–24, 1925 was to bring two hundred conventioneers to the Memphis Auditorium and Market on Front Street; the ADMA will have convention headquarters in the Baumgarten Hotel.

Janie will dress as a virginal eighteen-year-old and sit outside the Baumgarten and weep.

Her boyfriend will have taken her luggage and left her with no money or place to go. She will be exhausted and need someplace to lie down for an hour. Janie will mark a man in his forties to ask for help. He will take her up to his room, and Janie will make sure the door does not lock. After five minutes, Jakes and a photographer will break in catching a nude Janie in the arms of the Good Samaritan. Jakes will offer the pictures and negatives to the mark for four thousand dollars cash, or he will distribute them to the convention. The poor sucker will ante up, and the three extortionists will walk away with four thousand dollars.

"Police station, Sergeant Canyon," said answering Jake's call.

"Dale Rush. Connect me to Detective Dale Rush."

Jakes waited impatiently for three minutes.

"Rush here."

"Dale, tell me what happened to the girls."

"Damn, bad money turns up. Who are you talking about, Hubie?"

"You know who, the girls in the house on Mill Street that your blue-ass comrades shut down."

"Oh, *that* house. I'll tell you if you can get Janie for me. She enjoys her work."

"Yeah, at twenty years, she is one of the smartest girls Old Mabel had. How can I get Janie if I don't know where she is?"

"Twenty? Janie looks younger. She's in the Bevenus House for Wayward Girls. I didn't think little Janie was that wayward."

"Can I get her out without paying money?" Jakes asked.

"If you're her father or uncle and can prove it. You don't qualify."

"Want to bet?"

"No. Up to this point, you've lived a charmed life, but that's bound to change."

"Don't count on it. I've got plenty of juice left. Goodbye, Dale," Jakes said and mumbled under his breath, "You asshole."

Jakes borrowed a city street directory from the Red Lantern barkeep. He turned to the P's in the book searched with his finger and stopped at Pearl Bevenus House for Wayward Girls. He shouted, "Anybody got a pencil?"

One of the half-drunk railroad workers handed him a beat-up pencil stub. Jakes looked at it and nodded at what was left of the lead. He wrote "511," the street number, on the wall and returned with a piece of paper he had gotten from the barkeep. With the worn pencil, he carefully wrote the King Street address of Janie's wayward home.

Jakes drove carefully around the metal fence surrounding the building. The Pearl Bevenus Home for Wayward Girls was a prison, not a home. Getting Janie out of prison would be more difficult than slipping her out of a house. With confidence, he parked at the front gate and rang the bell to summon a guard.

"I want to visit my niece, Janie Adams," he told the guard.

"You wait here."

A big raw-bone woman along with the guard came to the gate and said, "I'm Warden Krist. What do you want?"

"My name is Hubert Simms, and I want to visit my niece, Janie Adams," Jakes said.

"We ain't got no Janie Adams."

"She's sixteen years old, five feet, three inches tall. Dark hair and brown eyes. One eye droops a bit."

"Yeah. We got a girl of that description, but her name ain't Adams."

"That's Janie. The poor girl started running with the wrong crowd and now, look where she is. Her mother sent me to look for her, and I checked at the Adams Street police station. A detective said a girl by Janie's description was in Pearl Bevenus Home. I can assure you that Janie didn't give her right name, but something she made up. I want to see her so I can tell her mother that she's in a safe place."

"Okay. Let him in," the warden told the guard, who opened the gate.

Jakes followed the warden through the buildings front door. It was almost like a dormitory except for the bars on all the windows. Warden Krist stopped at a small room off to the side of the long hall and motion to Jakes, "Wait here."

A few minutes later, the Warden followed by Janie came into the room. Jakes stood, and Janie ran to him and cried, "Uncle Clyde."

"I thought Hubert is your name?"

"It is. Hubert Clyde Simms. Janie always called me Clyde."

"I'll give you thirty minutes together, and that's all. I'll be back at that time."

Jakes and Janie listened for the warden's footsteps to fade before they began to talk.

"You promised us you'd take care of me if I did what you asked. That was a lie, you lousy scum. I have to stay here for a year."

"I am here to see if I can get you out. It will not be easy. Tell me everything that goes on from daylight to bedtime. I'll break you, and only you, out some way. What time do you get up every morning?"

"Six o'clock everyday six days a week. They let us sleep late on Sunday."

"What is your daily schedule?"

"School classes from eight o'clock to eleven o'clock. We make women's clothes in the afternoon. Simple dresses. They are learning us a trade. We can work in a clothing factory when we get out. The factories pay starvation wages."

"Is there a window without bars?" Jakes asked.

"No. They all have iron bars. But there is one window in a second story room that some girls dug out the cement around two bars. They were discharged before the job was finished. I'll ask the women who live in that room if the bars are loose and can be pulled out enough to get through. I'm skinny enough."

"Will the second floor be a problem?"

"I'll tie two sheets together and slide down to the ground."

"Will they want to go with you?"

"No, I know these girls. They are short timers and won't help or report me. They will pretend to sleep. Where am I going after I get out?"

"You'll work for me."

"I ain't gonna lay in my back if that's what you're thinking."

"You'll not be on your back for this one. You'll get undressed and put on a show."

"What do you mean, 'I'll get undressed.' I will not allow no one to rape me. You understand."

"We choose a mark. He will pick you up. Let him take you to his room, and I'll break in with a photographer. We sell the mark a set of prints for good amount of cash. We won't have to work this very long before we accumulate a good bit of money. We split the take three ways."

Jakes explained the set-up to her. "Now, check to see if you can break out. If you can, write a letter to your old uncle at this address. Say you are doing well and looking forward to an early discharge for good behavior. I'll write you back with an escape date the darkest night in August, one without a moon. In the letter I send will be the day and month in code. If you see something that costs 8.90, that means I will break you out on the night of August 9 at two in the morning. Go to the back fence, and I'll signal you where I cut the chain link. Don't bring anything with you. I'll have clothes and everything you need. Remember it is always two in the morning."

"Where will I stay?" Janie asked.

"In my Downing apartment the first night. Then, I'll rent a

house," Jakes said and heard footsteps coming down the hall.

"Time is up," the warden said.

"Oh, Uncle Clyde, I hate to see you go. Can you get me out of here?"

"I'm sorry, sweet Janie. You'll have to serve your time, but I'll visit you again. And will help you get started when you've paid your debt to the state."

Janie stood and hugged Jakes. With tears in her eyes, she said, "Bye, Uncle Clyde, I love you."

"Love you too, Janie." Jakes copped a feel while he held her.

The warden watched the goodbyes and thought how lucky Janie is to have a wonderful uncle to care for her.

Jakes left the prison with renewed energy. Now, he had a scheme with the potential to make real money to pay Ronny and have enough left over to leave Memphis after killing Detective Bill Bonner.

CHAPTER 47

MCBRIDE AND BONNER

The two Memphis detectives sat across the desk from each other. Crime business slowed down after Labor Day, and they were looking through cold-case files.

"There's nothing here," Bonner said. He put the folder on top of a stack of files.

Chief Roberts appeared and roared, "Get to work. It ain't Christmas, and you're not on vacation."

"We're working on cold-cases," Patrick said.

"Here's one that's hot," Roberts slid a complaint form in front Patrick. "See what you two ace detectives can do with that one."

Patrick read the complaint form and handed it to Bonner who scanned the document.

"It's the old dead-letter scam. Someone set up this lady after her husband died. The confidence man wrote a private letter to the deceased asking for payment of the money he lent him. The letter writer needed the money to pay for his wife's hospital bill. In their state of grieving, the family opens the letter and sends a check to the return address, which is a post office box. The con-man opens a bank account under an assumed name, and the check is cashed by the bank. The con-man walks out with cash in his pocket," Bonner told Patrick. "pretty slick operator."

"How do you catch this scammer?"

"He'll get away with it until the victims begin to complain. By then, he figures he has milked the cow dry. The only way to catch him is with his letter asking for the loan payment. If a potential victim knows his deceased husband or father didn't borrow money and brings us the letter, we can find him," Bonner said. "I hope one of our citizens is conscientious enough to bring the letter to us. We'll nail him."

"Is there anything we can do but wait?" Patrick asked.

"We can scan the obituary column and see who died in an upper-class neighborhood. That's how our friendly confidence man does it."

"Damn, that's morbid," Patrick said.

The detectives read the obituaries every day for two weeks.

"Bonner, this one sounds promising. Charles Hazlet, the owner of Hazlet Boat Company, passed away leaving a wife. No children, but one brother. He was sixty-five, so his wife can't be much younger. Sorrow at her age makes her an easy mark. Let's contact his brother today before the scammer writes the letter."

"If the Hazlets get a letter, we will have something to go on. Let's pay a visit to Gate's Funeral Parlor where old Hazlet lies in state," Bonner said.

"May I help you, gentlemen," Andy "Pearly" Gates asked.

"Yeah, Pearly," Patrick said. "We want to pay our respects to the Hazlet family."

Pearly said, "Shhh. Gentlemen, please. My name is Andy. Thanks for the business, Detective McBride. Come this way, gentlemen."

He led the two into the viewing room where Lottie, Charles Hazlet's wife, sat holding a lace handkerchief and Ed Hazlet, his brother, stood beside the coffin.

"Mr. Hazlet, these gentlemen would like to speak to you in private. Please use the weeping room at the end of the hall," Pearly said.

Patrick, Bonner and Ed Hazlet followed the undertaker to the small weeping room. At the door, Pearly stopped and motioned for the men to enter and silently left before Bonner thanked him.

"What do you want, detectives?"

"We think Mrs. Hazlet will get a letter from Charles Hazlet's friend that asks for repayment of a loan. The letter will pretend the writer doesn't know that Mr. Hazlet is deceased and will claim he is a friend who desperately needs the money. Using the excuse that his wife is in the hospital waiting for an expensive operation. He will ask for five hundred dollars or more.”

“I can’t believe anyone could stoop that low,” Ed Hazlet said.

“If Mrs. Hazlet gets a letter of this nature, please contact me or McBride, my partner. Maybe we can shut this scam down.”

“McBride? Where have I heard your name?” Ed Hazlet asked.

“It’s a common name on the police force. Irishmen dominate police departments,” Bonner said. “Call this number at the Adams Street police station.”

Hazlet took the card Bonner offered and said, “I will the minute a letter comes in.”

CHAPTER 48

Janie Is Out

Janie told Molly and Lois, the girls in the room with the loose bars, she intended to escape and asked for their help. Both swore to keep her secret and agreed to help by pretending sleep and hear nothing. Janie trusted them because they had a passionate hatred of Old Lady Krist and wanted to get her in trouble.

She didn't trust Ellen, her roommate, and told her nothing about the escape plan. She lifted two sheets from the laundry cart and hid them away. Janie tied the sheets together and measured them to make sure she could reach the ground from the second floor.

Janie noted the movements Krist and the guards made. They never varied the night patrol. One night she practiced slipping out of her room without waking her roommate. She visited the Molly and Lois to test the loose bars. She could pull one bar almost out, but the other needed to have the loose concrete dug out around the bar.

Janie stole a spoon from the kitchen and sharpen it to a fine edge. At night without help from Lois and Molly, she dug out the crumbling concrete with the spoon and eventually pulled the bar away from the window frame leaving enough space for her to squeeze through. Janie carefully prepared to escape at a minute's notice. She became impatient when August passed into September. Jakes' letter came on September twenty-four.

Janie read Jakes' letter carefully down to the code that told her on the night of September twenty-six there will be no moon and dark enough to risk a break. She hoped Jakes' great plan worked; it was worth all the trouble to get out of this so-called home for wayward girls.

Hubert Jakes is a slick back-stabber, and I'll go along with his extortion scam until I save enough money. But as soon as I can get away from him, I'll be gone, thought Janie as she put her escape plan in motion.

Janie rolled and folded the sheets and hid them in the locker under her bed. She slipped her only light nightgown over her head and didn't bother with underwear. She told her roommate goodnight at ten o'clock lights out, turned to face the wall and pretended to go to sleep. Janie was fortunate to have a roommate that went into a deep sleep soon after going to bed.

The two roommates had bought an alarm clock, and Janie would use it to good advantage. She didn't need an alarm; she wouldn't go to sleep but took stock of her life. Sent to juvenile prison at nineteen. She claimed to be sixteen when the cops loaded Old Mabel's girls into the paddy wagon. That kept her from seeing the inside of the Shelby County Women's prison.

She began turning tricks at sixteen; released from jail four times in as many years. She borrowed money from that old hag, Mabel, and couldn't pay it back. Mabel let her work off the debt on her back. Then, along came Hubert Jakes. He claimed her exclusive charms, and she kept him and his bed warm until a cop brought Old Mabel's house down. In a way, she felt relieved to be out of the life and vowed never to return.

There was one hall light in their section of the dormitory. Janie held the clock to see the time by dim hall light; it was one-thirty and time to go. Silently, she put her feet on the floor and brought out the sheets from under the bed. She walked down the hall to Lois and Molly's room; there were no locks on any of the dormitory doors. Janie went in.

"Is that you Janie?" Molly asked.

"Yeah. Time for me to get out of here. Stay in your bunk, I can do the sheets myself," she said and looped one end of the two tied together sheets around the stronger window bars. Her one hundred and ten pounds wouldn't put much strain on them. She played out the sheets until the end touched the ground.

By this time Lois and Molly were awake and pulling the loose bars apart. It took a bit of maneuvering because Janie had developed nicely up top. After she squeezed through, Janie took hold of the sheets with both hands.

"When I reach the ground, untie the sheets and let them fall. I'll take them with me and get rid of them. Goodbye, Molly. Goodbye, Lois. Thanks for all your help and good luck when you're free."

The two roommates said, "Goodbye and good luck to you, Janie."

The sheets dropped beside Janie as soon as she touched the ground. She gathered them up in her arms and quickly made her way to the fence where Jakes waited.

"Over here, Janie," Jakes whispered.

She pushed the sheets through the fence opening first and with the help of Jakes, squeezed through trying to keep him from copping a feel beneath her nightgown. He hurried her to his Overland, threw the sheets in the backseat, and helped Janie into the passenger seat.

At the entrance to the Downing Apartments, Jakes first turned off the headlamps of the Overland. When he got closer to the apartments, he cut the engine and coasted to a stop in his parking place. Janie pulled herself out of the Overland and joined Jakes. They were walking toward his apartment when Jakes stopped and held Janie back.

"Over there," he whispered and pointed to a figure of a man coming up the walk.

The man stopped and called, "Who are you and what are you doing out here at this time of night?"

"If it's any of your business, Mister, I'm telling my girl goodnight. So, go on your way and stop bothering people."

"Very well," Patrick McBride said and thought about showing his badge and demanding a better explanation but decided he had acquired the detective's skepticism and let it go.

Jakes let his breath out and hurried Janie into his apartment.

"You'll find your clothes in that closet," Jakes said and pointed to a closed door in the bedroom. Janie wanted to put something on her bare skin, rushed to the closet, and opened the door.

"You are a bastard, Hubert Jakes. You said you would furnish me with clothes. There is nothing in here but lingerie."

"That's all you need, Little Janie. I can't let you out until I've set up my money project. And, I like to see you walk around in your altogether."

"I'm sleepy and want to go to bed," Janie said.

"You can sleep in that bedroom," Jakes said, indicating the one with the clothes closet.

"Where's your bedroom.?"

"That *is* my bedroom. I thought we could take up where we left off," Jakes said with a grin.

"I'll sleep on the living room sofa," Janie said.

"Now, little Janie. Don't be naughty or I'll have to spank you."

"Do you go to sleep, Jakes?"

"So, what," he said.

"You better stay awake, or you'll wake up missing something very dear to you."

"You wouldn't do that, would you?"

"Try me and see, Hubie," Janie said.

"Okay. You sleep on the sofa."

Janie knew he was a coward and would not try to physically hurt her. She pledged to take advantage of his weakness. *First, I need clothes, and Jakes will get what I want within a day or so. Meanwhile, I'll bide my time.*

Janie heard Jakes leave at ten that morning. She wanted to enjoy, as much as she could, her freedom, so she went back to sleep. She woke up again at one o'clock, made coffee and fixed breakfast. Washed her nightgown in the sink and filled the bathtub with water. Janie relaxed in the tub for half an hour. She put on her panties and slipped on her nightgown.

Maybe I'll wear a pair of Jakes pants and go to a store. Then, she remembered she had no money. Janie begin to search drawers for cash Jakes had hidden. She picked up a pile of note paper and read what Jakes had written.

Leave for work: 8
Home from work: 5
To Bed at 10
No male visitor
Two nights per week out with girls

Has one quart of milk every other day
Has cereal with milk for breakfast
Ask chemist if chloral hydrate works in milk?
Milk put in the cold box
Milk in kitchen ice box
Iceman delivers every other day. 12 Apartment
Manager lets iceman have a master key?

Jakes plans to kidnap someone. *If I find out who, I'll have more power over him. He is organized, I concede that.*

Janie hadn't counted on being locked up in Jakes' house for three weeks. She almost wished she had not broken out of the home. She had to do something to convince him to let her out.

GREED, BANE OF CON MEN

Jakes' dead-letter scam brought in another thousand dollars. He needed the money before he began his extortion project. He could be pushing his luck trying to get away with one more dead-letter scam. Easy money convinced him to do it. He searched the newspaper obituaries and found the perfect mark: Charles Hazlet with a live widow, one brother, and no children. Jakes learned everything he could about Charles Hazlet. He discovered that Hazlet went to St Louis on business six months before his death. Hubie used this to increase the believability of the letter. He put the loan at a thousand dollars.

He wrote a letter to Charles Hazlet:

> I would not ask, but my wife is in the hospital with mounting medical bills that have drained my savings, and I need money badly. Please pay me the $1000 you borrowed for the emergency in St. Louis. I know I told you to pay me back in due time, but I genuinely need the money, now.
> Your Old Friend, Bob Owens

Jakes mailed the letter and marked the day the check would arrive. After the third day, he sent Levi to the mailbox.

Ed Hazlet called detective sergeant Bill Bonner. "I received a letter from Bob Owens wants payment of a loan for a thousand dollars. He said he made this loan in St. Louis when he and my brother were at a business meeting. The return address is box 126 at the main post office on Third Street.”

“Mail the check, and we’ll stake out the post office. The pickup man is not normally the con artist but will lead us to the mastermind,” Bonner told him. “If you mail it today, it will get to the main post office tomorrow and in the box by Thursday. We start tomorrow morning.”

“Consider the check mailed,” Ed Hazlet said.

Patrick listened to Bonner’s side of the conversation, and when he hung up the receiver, Patrick asked, “Who will stake it out.”

“You and I initially. I don’t think it will take that long for a letter to go to a post office box. You and I will take shifts tomorrow, just in case the letter arrives early.”

“It will be the first time the U.S. post office will have delivered something on time.”

Bonner stood first two-hour shift. He sat reading a newspaper on a bench outside the post office. Through a large window, he had a clear view of the boxes built into the inside wall with the mail sorters on the opposite side. It didn’t take long for Bonner’s back to begin hurting. He walked up and down in front of the post office then he returned to the bench.

“It has to be an easy job to sit around reading for two hours,” Patrick said when he stood in front of Bonner.

“Yeah, buster. See how easy it is for you. I’m going to take a nap. I leave you the reading material,” Bonner said, and carefully folded the newspaper.

Patrick counted ten Home Run cigarette butts at the end of the bench. Bonner had pinched the fire out and dropped them. He made a note to look for a blister on Bonner’s thumb and index finger. Patrick established himself as comfortable as possible on a cement bench and opened *Riders of the Purple Sage* to the page he marked months before and began to read. A shadow fell across his book and stopped. Patrick looked into the hard eyes of a scarred face.

“May I do something for you?” Patrick asked.

“Tell me why you sat here for an hour without moving.”

“I enjoy reading Zane Grey.”

"Do you have any identification?"

"I do. It's in my inside coat pocket," Patrick said and recognized a fellow cop. He took his badge out carefully and held it where the stranger could see it. "I'm on a stakeout. Watching box 126 for a letter to appear. We're trying to catch a con man working the dead-letter scam. And, you?"

"Gangsters. A tip came in that a gang out of Texas will hit this post office. It's probably nothing, but we follow up on every report. It's credible since there have been three post offices hit in the last three weeks. I'd like to help you, but my job is protecting the post."

"I understand. My sergeant thinks the letter, mailed last night could get here today. Odds are against delivery today."

"He could be right. Good luck," the federal cop said and walked back into the post office.

Foot traffic became busier. People begin checking boxes for mail. Patrick arose from the bench and stood to observe the P.O. box.

He saw a bum stagger up to box 126 and open it. He took out a letter and put it in his pocket. When he left the building, Patrick followed. The inebriated bum went into a drugstore a block from the post office. Patrick waited until he came out with a prescription bottle of alcohol. Patrick decided to grab him since he couldn't see inside the drugstore and it could have been a drop point.

Patrick stepped in front of the man and from his looks, identified him as a war veteran. "You're under arrest. Put your hands out, I have to handcuff you."

"I ain't done nothing. Why are you arresting me?"

"What do you have in your pocket?"

"A letter with a check for Mr. Owens. I'm his messenger and pick up his mail."

McBride signaled a patrol officer to come over.

"What is your name?"

"Levi."

"Take the envelope from your pocket and give it to me."

The patrolman joined them while Levi went into his pocket for the letter.

Levi gave the envelope to Patrick with a shaking hand. Patrick opened the letter and extracted a check signed made out to Owens and signed by Ed Hazlet. Patrick told the patrolman, "Call for someone to take this man to jail and tell Sergeant Roberts to get a message to Detective Bonner, that he's coming into the station."

"Come on, Levi. We might as well sit on the bench while we wait." McBride didn't follow protocol and left the old soldier unhandcuffed. The paddy wagon arrived thirty minutes later, and the officers handcuffed Levi and loaded him into the vehicle. The luncheon crowd watched the wagon disappear down Union Street.

Bonner was sitting in the holding cell facing Levi when Patrick arrived at the station. The interrogation had begun.

"Who hired you to be their messenger?" Bonner asked.

"Mr. Owens."

"Levi, we know Mr. Owens doesn't exist. Who hired you?"

"That check is made out to Mr. Owens. and he hired me."

"Describe Mr. Owens?"

"He's about this high." Levi used his hand and arm to show the man's height, "He is skinny."

"What color are his eyes?" Bonner asked.

"I don't know. Brown, maybe."

"And his hair?"

"That's easy, silver gray. He's an old man, but he still looks good for his age."

"Okay, that's enough for now. We'll have to hold you for a short time, Levi. I'll take you back to your cell," Bonner said.

"Will I get something to eat?"

Patrick sat at his desk in the detective squad room when Bonner entered and before Patrick asked, Bonner answered, "It's Hubert Jakes. Perfect description. He's close, and I can find him this time."

"I thought he was smarter than to get caught in this scheme. He may need money to leave Memphis," Patrick said.

"I doubt that. Memphis is a gold mine for cons and scams. Jakes pushes harder because he thinks he is so smart that he'll never be caught. I'll put the word on the street. Maybe a snitch will turn up something."

EXTORTION BY PHOTOGRAPH

After a month, Hubert Jakes opened his apartment door and called. "Janie. I'm home. Come out, come out wherever you are."

Janie came out of the bedroom nude and pranced around Jakes. "Get me some clothes, Jakes or I'll tell you-know-who about you spying."

"What are you talking about?"

"Don't be coy. Does number twelve refresh your memory."

"You've snooped in my private business. This time I will spank you," Jakes said and started for Janie. She was ready with a swift kick in the groin. Hubie fell gasping for breath.

"Damn you, Janie," he croaked. "I'll get you just like I'll get little Miss Bitch Millicent Blanchard."

"You don't try that with me, Hubie. And if you don't get me clothes soon, while you leave me locked up, I'll destroy those fancy suits you wear."

"Okay. I'll get a couple of skirts and blouses for you this afternoon."

Jakes left to find a down-and-out photographer to take extortion pictures of Janie and the mark. He found Gene Wonders in a speakeasy on River Street.

"Gene Wonders. I haven't seen you in a coon's age. How you doing?"

"Just getting by, Hubie. No one will hire me since the editor of the newspaper caught me taking porn pictures. I told him they was art, but he would not listen and fired me and blackballed me in Memphis."

"If you're interested, I have a job for you. It won't last long, but it will be lucrative."

"Is it dangerous."

"No. It is a little bit outside the law."

"It's one of your cons. Like the ones you ran years ago?"

"The old, catch-the guy-with-his-arms-around-naked-young-girl con."

"Okay, I'll go with you. Who is the girl?"

"Remember Janie?"

"I can never forget Janie. She's perfect."

"Come to my apartment tomorrow at eleven in the morning. It's apartment nine."

Jakes brought two outfits, a cute teenage girl's skirt and blouse and an old woman's outfit. After they photographed the mark, Janie could walk out with an older look. He accomplished two things, procured a photographer and made Janie happy. Jakes was pleased with himself. He was all business when he went into his apartment.

"Here are two skirts and two blouses for you," he said and tossed the bags to Janie.

"Hubie, you are a real piece of horse manure. These are work clothes. I want something myself for myself. You're trying to keep me from going out, and you better get that out of your lousy head."

"Why are you so upset. I bought you clothes."

"You are right. I have clothes now," Janie said and became more suspicious. She knew he intended to do something to her, and she had to keep one step ahead of him.

At eleven o'clock the next morning, photographer Gene Wonders knocked on the door, Janie saw him through the peephole and opened the door.

"Hi, Janie," said Gene.

"Hello. How's the pornography business."

"I could make a lot of money if I could take pictures of you."

"Jakes is still asleep. You can wake him."

"You wore him out last night," Gene said with a snicker.

"Gene, don't put me in the bed with that rat. If it's any of your business, I sleep on the sofa."

"I'll wake Jakes," he said and entered Jakes bedroom.

"Janie, damn it, you didn't wake me up. Get me a cup of coffee."

"Get it yourself. I'm not your servant."

"You were last night," Jakes said and grinned at Gene.

Gene laughed, "Did you sleep on the sofa?"

Jakes didn't answer. He brought a cup of coffee out of the kitchen.

CHAPTER 52

MILLICENT BLANCHARD'S THANKSGIVING

Thoughts of Patrick McBride bothered Millicent Blanchard through Thanksgiving dinner and that night. She told her father she needed to go back to Memphis on Saturday to meet with her co-workers at St. Anthony's which was partially true. Betty Jean and Julia were going to a play on Saturday evening. They asked Millicent to go, but she wanted to spend the weekend in Arkansas. Now, she had second thoughts, not knowing why she wanted to see Patrick McBride.

Saturday morning, her father drove her to Helena, Arkansas dock where she caught a riverboat to Memphis. She called Patrick at home. The telephone rang several times before McBride picked up.

"Hello."

"Patrick? This is Millicent. I came back from Arkansas to talk with you. Will you meet me at the Meridian for coffee and pie?"

"Yes, I'll meet you. When?"

"In fifteen minutes?"

"I'll be there."

Patrick had been working on a sticky drawer in one of his cupboards, so he changed his work clothes into a more appropriate suit and drove his Moon down to the Meridian Café. November weather had turned cold, and he wore his detective's overcoat.

Millicent stood inside and saw him drive up. She ran out the Café door and flung her arms around McBride's waist. He was taken surprised at her actions but responded by holding her close.

"Why am I lonesome without you?"

"I can't answer that. We haven't known each other that long and haven't been together very much."

"I had an empty place in my heart at Thanksgiving dinner and yearned to see you. Don't stop holding me, please."

"Do you really want coffee and dessert?"

"No. I want to be with you."

"Could we go to your apartment?"

"Let's."

Ten minutes later Millicent and Patrick were sitting side by side on the couch in her living room. Neither could understand the feeling between them. She wanted his arms around her but didn't ask. Patrick's mourning period was over. That didn't release him from the memory of his love for Laura. He hadn't looked for nor found the woman to love and make him happy. He had to tell Millicent his story.

"I fell madly in love with Laura Hemphill. She said that she fell in love when she first saw me. I was on my way to Texas until she changed my life. After our first encounter, she hunted and found me walking a police beat. I remember telling her about my determination to leave Memphis after a year on the force, and I didn't have anything in Memphis. She said to me I didn't realize how much I had in Memphis. On Christmas Day I volunteered to take two shifts so one of the married men could be home with his family. It snowed and turned cold. I walked my beat and heard the frozen snow crunching beneath my feet. I thought of Laura with every step. It hit me like a rifle shot, I loved the girl. The snow and cold didn't affect me. When I came home after my tour of duty, she had steak and potatoes waiting for me. I asked her to marry me Christmas night 1923. She planned our wedding for April. She became sick with what we thought was the flu. She died of a blood disease last March. I do not mourn now, but the memory—the memory won't let me be until I find someone that will make it happen."

Millicent sat quietly listening. She tried to stem the tears without success. "That's a beautiful story, and I'm so sorry about Laura. Does this mean I have no chance with you?"

"I like you. You're funny and a beautiful person. I cannot answer you now and don't know when I can. So, don't wait for me. I just don't know." The image of Beth came into his mind. She was the other woman he could not erase from his memory. Maybe it was that way with first loves, and he did love her deeply. Laura's love made him put Beth aside. At times when he did remember Beth, he felt guilty and dismissed the memory.

"Can we continue our friendship and our supper once a week?"

"I'd like nothing better. I've bent your ear too long and must go."

Millicent didn't try to convince him to stay longer. She helped him with his coat and walked him to the door. He turned to say good night. Millicent stood on her tiptoes and kissed him passionately and said, "That's for being you." She gently closed the door before he could answer.

A man stood at Patrick's apartment door. He slipped his hand into his coat and held his weapon lightly.

"May I help you, sir?" Patrick asked.

"Yes. I believe this is a Patrick McBride's apartment. I have traveled a long way to deliver a package to him." the man spoke with a British accent.

"I'm Patrick McBride."

"My name is Cecil Palmer from the Gibbon's Detective Agency, Birmingham, England. I've looked for you in the States for two months. Colonel Gadsden Formstone left this package to be delivered after his death. Unfortunately, we discovered it three months ago. I hope it's not too late, and if it is, please accept my sincere apologies."

"Colonel Formstone sent this? He's been dead for more than two years."

"Do you have any identification, sir? Before I release the package, I have to verify that you are Patrick McBride."

McBride took his Memphis Police badge from his inside coat pocket and showed it to Palmer. "Will this suffice?"

"Indeed, it will. Please sign this release. This is an affidavit that delivered the package."

The Memphis Detective signed the paper and Cecil Palmer handed him the small package.

"Thank you, Mr. Palmer. Safe journey home," McBride said.

He looked at the package and thought *Colonel Formstone left this for me before he died.* He remembered Formstone saying the colonel would find some way to show his appreciation.

Inside his apartment, Patrick carefully opened the package and peeled layered wrapping paper away from a small case with an attached letter. He opened the envelope and extracted the paper.

Patrick read:

> Patrick, please accept this gift as appreciation for your sacrifice. Inside you will find two rings. I gave these to my wife and promised her to give them to Beth. Use it to bond my dear Beth to you. I relinquish my control from her life and know she will be in the best of care with you.
> Your Friend,
> Colonel Gadsden Formstone.

He opened the box and found two rings. An engagement and a wedding band. Tears formed in his eyes when he thought, *a bit too late, but thank you colonel.*

BETH DECIDES TO MARRY PHILIP

Beth went to Hawkins and Hawkins Law offices from the train. She knocked on Philip's door and heard him say, "Come!" Beth sat down in Philip's leather easy-chair.

"I didn't accomplish anything in Liverpool," she said. "Even if I go to the States, odds of ever finding him will be against me."

"Beth Formstone, marry a flesh and blood man who loves you and will never leave you. That's me."

He is here, and God only knows where Patrick is. I do love Philip, and maybe my love will grow after we're married.

"Yes. I will marry you. Philip."

Philip pulled Beth to her feet from the leather chair and kissed her. She returned his kiss.

"When do you want to set the date?" He asked not wanting her to have second thoughts.

"I'll have to look at a calendar and find a suitable month. I love Christmas. How about December sixth? It's a lovely month, and we won't have to decorate," Beth said.

"Excellent idea."

Glenda Wheeler and Megan Rakestraw, Beth's friends from the law office, volunteered to help with the wedding plans. Beth put Glenda in charge of arranging a prewedding party. Megan had the job of finding a small combo to play popular songs.

Beth and Philip decided on a civil ceremony since neither practiced his or her religion.

"It's faster and not as expensive as a church wedding, and the knot will be as tight if we took our vows in a church," Philip said.

Beth agreed. Beth agreed with all of Philip's wedding arrangements. He didn't notice her lack of enthusiasm. Beth didn't care. She wanted to have it over so she could get on with her life.

Philip set Friday, December fifth as the wedding date without consulting Beth. Solicitor Ralph Hawkins sponsored a pre-wedding party for the couple. Glenda Wheeler agreed to hire a room in the Shrewsbury Castle for the wedding party on December third, two days before the wedding.

Glenda Wheeler asked to see the Shrewsbury Castle rental agent.

"One moment please," the receptionist said and called the agent over an intercom.

"It's a small affair," Glenda explained to the rental agent. "We'll begin at five o'clock. We will have drinks and hors d'oeuvres. By that time expect most of those invited will have arrived. Dinner will be served at six. After dinner our hosts, Ralph Hawkins will lead the guests in a series of toasts. We should be out by seven thirty."

"You have everything ready and timed," the agent said.

Glenda continued, "The Freddy Miller Combo will play during the social time and stop when dinner is served."

"I hope not that jazz music if you can call it music," the agent said.

"We requested the band play popular music, classic and new tunes."

"Excellent, we look forward to having Colonel Formstone's widow celebrate her upcoming wedding in the castle."

A week before the wedding party Beth became listless, Glenda and Megan attributed it to wedding blues. Beth didn't know why. She put Patrick out of her mind and hadn't thought of him during preparation for the event in December. In the past week, Beth slept fitfully and when waking remembered snatches of dreams of Patrick. She dismissed this as the aftermath of her abortive attempt to find him.

"Are you excited about your wedding," Ralph Hawkins asked Beth.

"Yes. Of course, I am," Beth said and smiled her enchanting smile.

In his forty years as a lawyer, Ralph Hawkins had seen almost every emotion a person could have. He sensed something wrong with Beth. Maybe it is premarital jitters. But his depth of experience dealing with clients gave Hawkins an uneasy feeling about Philip and Beth. And he didn't like what he felt.

"Philip tells me you two are leaving this weekend for a honeymoon in Spain," Ralph Hawkins said to Beth.

"Yes. I've never been, but Philip said it is wonderful. I am sure I'll love Spain."

"Beth, I understand your search for the young American didn't turn up a trace. I know you are disappointed, but Philip is very much enamored of you and will make a good husband. A bird in the hand is much better than a bird in an American bush," Hawkins said and chuckled.

"Yes, he will be a good and kind husband, and I do love him," she said.

"But?" Hawkins posed the question.

"I will marry him, and we will be happy here in Shrewsbury."

"Excellent," said Hawkins with more enthusiasm than he felt.

Beth believed she did love Philip and her love for him would grow without a doubt. She looked forward to wearing the dress Megan help select for the party. The long navy-blue velvet fitted Jersey V-Neck dress emphasized her figure and highlighted her dark-blonde hair. Although the dress was beautiful, a reluctant Beth bought the dress on Megan's suggestion. She knew more about fashion than the-bride-to-be.

"This dress will make Kelly's eyes pop," said Megan.

"I'm positive he will approve," she replied.

Philip called for Beth at her home in Wem to take her to the party.

"My God, you're beautiful," Philip said when Beth opened the door.

"I hope I'm not over-dressed. I feel conspicuous," Beth said.

"You shouldn't. I approve. It's almost five o'clock. we must be going." Philip helped her into his Crossley.

On the way to the castle, Beth thought if she were marrying Patrick, would she feel the same as she feels now. She didn't have an answer to that question and wasn't likely to ever get one. Beth thanked her lucky stars that she had packed for the honeymoon. At this point, she didn't want to go to Spain. She would never let Philip know how she felt.

At ten minutes after five o'clock, Philip parked the car in a designated area and helped Beth out. They recognized several guests' cars, and Philip said, "We'll make our grand entrance and greet everyone. If my lawyer friends have arrived, the hors-d'oeuvres will be eaten already."

When the couple entered the party room, all chatter ceased, and the room became quiet. One of Philip's friends whistled. Ralph Hawkins broke the silence.

"Let's welcome this lovely couple," he said. Guests applauded. Beth thought how shy Patrick had been and felt the same in this situation.

Philip's friends gathered around the couple.

"Philip, you don't deserve this beautiful woman. Let me take her off your hands."

"Yeah. Beth, this old boy doesn't know how lucky he is. Your presence lights up the room."

"May I bring you a plate of hors-d'oeuvres, Beth?"

"No, thank you. I'll wait for dinner."

Ralph Hawkins saw the young men buzzing around Beth like a swarm of bees and went to her rescue. "Will you join Minnie and me for a few minutes?"

After making her excuses, she followed Hawkins back to a table where his wife and other wives of members of the law firm were sitting.

"Thanks, Mr. Hawkins. I don't think I could have taken much more of how beautiful I am. Hello, Mrs. Hawkins."

"You are beautiful, Beth. Don't deny it," Mrs. Hawkins said.

Beth Formstone didn't see herself as beautiful or even pretty, and it embarrassed her to be called beautiful. She knew men and women were drawn to her but didn't think looks had anything to do with it. Beth believed she projected a kind, understanding personality that led to her attraction. That's how she attracted Patrick.

Philip came to the table and said, "I come to claim my bride and introduce her to a potential client. Come, darling."

That is the first endearing name Philip has called me. Patrick called me "sweetheart," "dear," and "darling."

Philip took her hand and led her to a table where two men sat. A ruddy, older gentleman and a younger man that favored the old man.

"Gentlemen, meet Beth Formstone, my bride-to-be. Beth, this is Robert Jenkins and Captain Bob, his father."

"I've heard very good things about you, Miss Formstone," Robert said.

"Very nice meeting you," the elder Jenkins said.

"I believe I've heard your name, Mr. Jenkins," Beth said to the father.

"I think not. Unless you've been in the shipping business. I'm retired now, but I commanded merchant ships for forty years."

"What ships?" Asked Beth.

"The old *Bristol Star* out of Liverpool was my last," he said.

Beth took a deep breath and slowly let it out. "Do you remember a young man that booked passage on your ship in Autumn, 1922, an American?"

"Aye, that I do. The crew tried to cheer up the sad young fellow. He lost the only girl he ever loved and talked about her all the way to Savannah. My first mate told him there were many fish in the sea, and he will find another to love."

"Do you remember his name? Could it have been McBride? Patrick McBride?" Beth asked.

"It *was* Patrick McBride. I remember it because he had the worst case of lovesickness that I have ever seen," Captain Jenkins said and looked at Beth intensely. "You're not the lass he mooned about for seven days? And I'll bet many, many more. He lives in Tennessee. I never heard him say what town."

"I am that girl."

"Too bad he lost you. Philip has quite the catch," the captain said.

Philip interrupted, "We must say hello to Mr. and Mrs. Littlefield. Thank you for celebrating with us." Philip took Beth's hand and led her toward another table filled with his clients.

The Freddy Miller Combo played the first notes of "Roses of Picardy" and the tenor began:

Roses are shining in Picardy,
In the hush of the silver dew,
Roses are flow'ring in Picardy,
But there's never a rose like you!

And finishes the song with:

But there's one rose that dies not in Picardy,
'Tis the rose that I keep in my heart.

Beth stopped, listened to the song, looked at Philip and said, "I can't go through with our wedding, Philip. I am so sorry, but my heart is with Patrick McBride, wherever he is."

Beth turned away from Philip and walked to the Hawkins' table. Ralph Hawkins sensed what had happened when she approached his table.

"Mr. Hawkins, will you please take me home," Beth asked.

"Yes. I will," and said to his wife, "Let's get Beth home. She has a long journey ahead and is anxious to begin."

"I must get Mrs. Peploe," Beth said.

Ralph Hawkins let Beth and Mrs. Peploe out at Beth's cottage.

"If you will be so kind as to wait for me to change into traveling togs and get my bags. I need a ride to the train station," Beth said.

"Of course, we'll take you there. How long will it take to pack your luggage?"

"They are ready. I packed my bags for the honeymoon, and I'll be back in five minutes."

A smiling Beth came out of the house. She had changed into traveling clothes and carried two suitcases. Mrs. Peploe trailed behind. "I'll take good care of the cottage while you're gone. Write as soon as you get to America."

To his wife, Hawkins said, "She is beautiful, isn't she?"

Hawkins help load the luggage into the car boot.

"I will write," Beth said and hugged the old lady.

"You look quite happy, Beth," Mrs. Hawkins said on the way to the train station.

"I am. At last, I will find my Patrick in America."

248

"Do you have money?" The Hawkins asked when he deposited Beth and her luggage at the depot.

"Yes. I kept cash on hand for an emergency. I'll be alright for the time being, but I'll have you wire money if I need it."

"Best of luck. And write us when you land," Hawkins told her and said to his wife, "See, my intuition was right on about this one."

Beth bought a one-way ticket to Liverpool and waited impatiently for the evening train.

HUBERT JAKES TAKES REVENGE

Jakes decided it was time to settle the score and rid himself of Detective Bill Bonner once and for all. He would show Ronny "Loose Change" Butts that he could use a pistol as well as a cop. Jakes had been secretly practicing firing his .38 Smith & Weston revolver. After weeks of practice, he could group four shots in a target circle. The Riverside beat was one of the longest of all Memphis beats, and one patrolman covered the entire strip. Dumbass Rush told him that Bonner and McBride had duty on Tuesday night. He did not intend to challenge Bonner but ambush him.

If Crazy McBride is with him, Jakes would take care of him too. Jakes became more confident with the use of a lethal weapon, and with excitement, he anticipated shooting and killing a man. He also thought about getting Ronny Butts before he had to pay the S.O.B. any more of his hard-earned money.

With the turmoil of trying to find the killer of two detectives, he'd have no trouble working his extortion scheme. By the end of January next year, Little Janie will bring in enough cash for him to disappear from Memphis and never come back. He laughed at his plans for Janie and Gene Wonders.

They will be surprised when I leave them holding the bag. I'll make Detective Dale Rush a hero for catching those extortionists. Little Miss Millicent Bitch Blanchard will not feel my ire. She should consider herself lucky that Old Hubie is leaving.

Jakes looked at his watch. Eleven o'clock. The weather turned cold and begin to sleet. He wore a heavy overcoat with a collar that turned up to keep his neck warm, a wool fedora that shed rain and sleet and hid his face. He parked the Overland next to a loading area where stevedores offloaded merchandise from riverboats and loaded waiting trucks. Weeks before he hunted for the perfect place for an ambush. He found it on the loading dock stacked high with palettes of machinery. It wasn't patrolled regularly. One old night watchman stayed in a shack and slept. One patrolman walked the long beat with a call box in the middle.

Jakes saw the patrolman coming down Riverside hunched against the sleet and watched him go by.

The patrolman quickly walked up to the call box and called the duty desk sergeant, Lusk. "Sarge, better send the detectives down to the loading dock. A dead woman is laying down hear. I'll stay by the body until they get here."

The sergeant walked back to the detective squad room where Bonner and Patrick sat at their desks reading.

"Hey, Bonner, McBride. Patrolman Hanson called in a dead body at the loading dock. You get down there and investigate. Hanson will be there. He is new, and I don't want to call out a bunch of men if he is seeing things, not there, in this weather," Lusk told them.

Bonner put out a Home Run by pinching the fire and threw it in the wastebasket.

"Why us?" Patrick asked.

"Isn't it always us," Bonner answered while slipping into his overcoat.

Patrick put on his coat and hat and followed Bonner out the door to the Model T.

"You drive," Bonner said.

"I bet your old fingers are stiff from the cold? You need something to warm them."

"Yeah, I get it later," Bonner said and slipped on his gloves.

Patrick stopped the police car on the street near the docks.

"Sarge said Hanson would be waiting here," Patrick said.

"Maybe on the other side of those palettes," said Bonner and Patrick began walking down the side of the palettes. The sleet had slacked off and not obstructing the detectives' vision as before.

McBride saw a figure step from behind the stacked machinery.

"Bonner, get down," Patrick shouted and pushed his partner aside. He pulled his gun from the shoulder holster but not fast enough. Patrick felt the .38 slug hit him and turn him around. The last thing he remembered before passing out was two shots. And then, three more.

Bonner had a hard time removing his gloved hand and drawing his .45 Smith & Weston. Jakes got off two shots but missed.

"You're going to die, Bonner," Jakes shouted.

That was his mistake. Bonner fired two rapid shots at the sound of Jakes' voice. He heard a grunt but no other sound. Bonner waited and listened for a sound from Jakes. There was none. He walked over to where Jakes lay, backed up ten feet, and fired another shot into Jakes' body.

Patrol Officer Hanson ran up to where he heard the shots fired and saw Bonner checking Patrick for a pulse.

"Call an ambulance, Hanson, *now*. My partner is still alive. Go! Go!"

Bonner felt under his overcoat for the gunshot wound and found it just above his heart. He pulled a handkerchief from his pocket and held it against the bleeding wound. It seemed like an hour for the ambulance to arrive, but it was only five minutes. The cold helped slow the bleeding.

By the time the ambulance arrived, five uniforms formed a cordon round Patrick to keep newspaper reporters away.

The ambulance attendants loaded Patrick into the ambulance and left in a rush urged on by Bonner who rode with Patrick.

CHAPTER 54

MCBRIDE SURVIVES

The emergency room doctors went to work stabilizing, removing the fragments of lead, cleaning and stitching his wound. Bonner would not leave the operating room. In no uncertain terms, the doctors told him to leave the operating room.

"Make me," he opened his coat and showed his .45, "I will not get out. I don't want you to screw up and kill my partner."

He watched the doctors work for two hours. When they took Patrick to the recovery room, Bonner paced the hospital hall with lit Home Run cigarettes. He pinched the fire end out without wetting his fingers. Chief Sergeant Flaherty and Patrolman Albert Sidney sat and watched Bonner.

Finally, the doctor came into the waiting room with a sour face. The three waited for the official verdict.

"There is no permanent damage," the doctor said. "The bullet missed the detective's heart by a hair, or you would be at the morgue, now. His heavy overcoat button diverted the bullet and shaved off shards of lead that fragmented throughout the right chest area. It missed his heart. He's visiting Morpheus now. He'll sleep for four or five hours, come back tomorrow morning,"

"Damn, I almost got my partner killed," Bonner said.

"How so?" Sergeant Flaherty asked.

"Hubert Jakes shot him instead of me. McBride pushed me out of the way and took the bullet. We've looked for Jakes for months, and he always got away. We need to let McBride's folk know about his wounds."

"He has no relatives," Albert Sidney said. "He is close to a couple in Kingsport."

"Does anybody know who they are or how we can contact them?" asked Bonner.

"Judge Webster or his wife will know. I'll call in the morning," Flaherty said.

"How about the Wednesday dinner date? Anyone know her?" Albert Sidney asked.

"What dinner date? He's been holding out on his partner," Bonner said.

Two uniforms came in, and Flaherty asked, "What are you doing here?"

"Sergeant Lusk sent us down; orders from Chief Flynn. He said to stay by McBride until we're relieved."

Bonner looked around at Albert Sidney and Flaherty, "I'm going for breakfast at Big Town, sack out on their cot, and be back in the morning. I want to be here when McBride wakes up to give him hell for what he did."

"I'm old, folks, and need my sleep, I'm going home," Sergeant Flaherty said.

"I'll stick around for a while, just in case," Albert Sidney said. He listened to Patrick mumble and pulled his chair closer to hear.

"Beth. I love you, Beth. I never forgot you. Why did you forget me?"

The next morning, Bonner, Albert Sidney and Sergeant Flaherty were watching him.

"Now, I know he's crazy. He kept mumbling 'Beth, Beth. I love you'," Albert Sidney told them.

The three policemen look around at the commotion at the door.

"He's my boyfriend. Let me through."

"I sorry, miss. We have orders to keep everyone out," the uniform said.

"It's okay. Let her through," Flaherty ordered.

Millicent pushed a guard away and rushed to Patrick's bedside bent over and kissed his brow.

"Are you Beth?" Albert Sidney asked.

"No, I wish I were. We're friends. He told me that Beth was his first love. Poor Patrick will never again see Beth, and now, this happens."

"I thought he had something going with his Wednesday dinner date," Albert Sidney said.

"I gave up when he told me that he is going to England to find Beth," said Millicent. "When he wakes, please tell him Millicent Blanchard came to see him, I'll come back after work."

HMS Mauretania To America

After running out on Philip, Beth felt sorry for him. But she knew shouldn't after he showed her off as a trophy to his clients. She had suspected he would use her to further his career and her fortune would also help him.

Beth arrived in Liverpool late that night, booked a room at the Adelphi Britannia. She spent a sleepless night in the room and arose early the morning of December fourth. She waited at the Cunard building entrance until a clerk opened the door.

"When does the next ship leave for America?" She asked at the ticket agent.

"*Mauretania.* She leaves tomorrow morning for New York, and we have cabins available," he answered.

"I'll book a cabin for one. I care not where it is located."

"Very good, miss," he said and began to fill out the ticket to America.

During the five-day crossing to New York City, Beth walked the deck day and night like a restless ghost. She made polite conversation with fellow passengers. Two young men asked her to attend a dance in the ballroom; they were disappointed when she told them that she will be married in America. Beth didn't talk about herself to her fellow passengers, and she remained a mystery. They saw her walking the deck at night and called her "the phantom."

The *Mauretania* docked in New York on Thursday, December tenth. After Beth went through customs, a taxi took her to the Commodore Hotel. She checked in and after a light dinner, sat at the room desk and planned the next move. Captain Jenkins confirmed he went back home to Tennessee. If Patrick had not left Tennessee, she would find him there, and Nashville, the capital city, is a good starting point.

Beth was up and ready to go by nine o'clock the next morning. She asked the concierge to make a reservation on the next train to Nashville, Tennessee. He told her the train left at twelver forty-five. She took a taxi to Union Station and boarded *The City of Memphis*. After settled in a compartment, she tried reading the *Saturday Evening Post* but none of the stories interested her. She went to the dining car, sat by a window and ordered tea.

A woman traveling alone is a target for men. Traveling salesmen are notorious for attempting to entice women into their compartment. Lindsey Few was one of those enticers and sat down in the seat across from Beth.

"Hi, little lady. I'm Lindsey Few. Where have you been all my life?"

"I'm going to meet my husband. He's a Nashville policeman. I'm sure he can tell you where I've been during your short life."

Mr. Few slipped out of his seat and walked to the back of the car. Beth breathed a sigh of relief. She could not keep still and walked between the club car and the dining car and back to her compartment where she finally settled in and went to sleep, fully dressed.

"Nashville, Nashville. In ten minutes," the conductor announced,

Beth gave a two-dollar tip to the conductor to have a porter unload her bags onto the platform. She was ready to exit before *The City of Memphis* slowed to a stop. The porter carried her bags to a taxi stand. She told the taxi driver to take her to the best hotel in Nashville. He dropped her off at General Jackson. At the counter, the clerk asked how long she intended to stay.

"I don't know. Maybe a day or two," Beth answered. A hotel bellman showed her to her room and left her two bags on a luggage rack. She hadn't bathed since disembarking from the ship, she drew water into a tub and soaked for an hour. The hot bath relaxed her, and she went to bed.

All the travel and worry caught up with her. Beth woke, up ravenously hungry, at seven o'clock the next morning. She took the elevator to the first floor, entered the hotel dining room and chose a table near a window. The waiter wrote her order of toast and tea on a pad.

Beth picked up a copy of the *Nashville Banner* that someone left in the chair next to her. She scanned the front page and opened to page two to "News from Around Tennessee" section. Her heart sank to the pit of her stomach when she recognized the name, McBride, in an AP story. Beth read:

December 12
Memphis Detective Shot.
An assailant shot Detective Patrick McBride who took a bullet to save the life of Sgt. Detective Bill Bonner, his partner. Bonner subsequently shot and killed Hubert Jakes, the assailant. McBride is recovering in Memphis General Hospital from the near-fatal wound.

Beth Formstone tried not to cry as she ate half her toast and swallowed a little tea. She hurriedly put money on the table for the food. Almost running to the front desk, she asked when did the next train leave for Memphis.

"Twelve-fifteen." the front desk clerk told her.

She arrived at the Nashville depot two hours early and paced in and out of the waiting room. The stranger asked, "Could I help you, miss?"

"The man I love may be dying in a Memphis Hospital. If you can get me to bloody Memphis before this train, yes."

"I'm sorry. I wish I could."

The train chugged out Nashville Station at twelve-twenty. Beth boarded the train and sat in a passenger seat urging the locomotive to go faster. She fidgeted for four-and-a-half hours.

BETH FINDS PATRICK

During the entire trip to Memphis, Beth prayed she could get to her darling and be at his side. She exited the train and had a porter take her bags to a locker in the depot. On the street, taxis sat in a cue waiting for a fare. Beth chose the first in line, opened the back door and slid in.

"How many hospitals are in Memphis?" she asked the driver.

"One," he said.

"Take me there."

When they arrived, Beth dropped two dollars in the front seat next to the driver, opened the door. and sprinted into Memphis General Hospital, leaving the driver confused but grateful for the tip.

She rushed to the nurses station and asked if Patrick McBride had left the hospital.

"No, he hasn't. He is still recovering from his wound."

"What is his room number?" Beth asked.

"Are you a relative?"

"Yes, I'm his wife."

A hefty nurse stood to the side to listen to the conversation. "You are not his wife. Mr. McBride never married after his fiancée died. So, who are you with an English accent?"

"Beth Formstone, if he hasn't forgotten me, I'll marry him," Beth answered.

Nurse Bradshaw said, "Mr. McBride has been unconscious for some time. He keeps calling for Beth. That was a surprise. He was engaged to Laura. Follow me to his room."

She followed Nurse Bradshaw down the hall restraining herself from screaming to get on with it. She knew it was his room when she saw two policemen standing at a room door.

"I can't let you in, lady," said a guard.

"Just try to keep me away from the man I'm going to marry," Beth said.

Another policeman came to the door and asked, "Who are you, ma am?"

"Beth Formstone."

Albert Sidney said to the guard, "Let her in. He's been waiting for Beth." And to Beth, "He is coming out of a morphine induced sleep. The doctor stopped the morphine last night. He's out of danger now."

Beth quietly slipped passed Albert Sidney and sat in the chair beside Patrick's bed. She took his hand and held it to her cheek. Patrick stirred.

"How long has he been here?" She asked.

"One day, two nights," he said and took a long look at Beth. *How does Patrick do it? She's even prettier than Laura.*

"Okay, Albert Sidney Smith. You can go back to work," Sergeant Flaherty said coming into Patrick's room followed by Sgt. Bonner.

"Gentleman, meet Detective Patrick McBride's future wife, Miss Beth Formstone. I must go to the ramparts and protect the citizenry, fare thee well, lovely lady."

"Are you the one he's called for the last two nights?" Flaherty asked. "I'm David Flaherty, and this is Detective Sergeant Bill Bonner, McBride's partner. I'm glad to see you and know you're real. I began to think you were a figment of his morphine imagination."

"My pleasure, ma'am," Bonner said with his intimidating grin.

"Does he act like that all the time?" Beth asks indicating Albert Sidney.

"He's McBride's best friend," Flaherty said.

"I'm glad you are here," Bonner said, "I'm getting tired of keeping McBride out of trouble, he needs a woman to care for him."

"If he wants me, I am here to stay," Beth said.

"If he doesn't want a woman who loves him enough to travel thousands of miles across sea and land, I'll have him committed into our local asylum," said Bonner.

Beth squeezed Patrick's hand, and he moved.

"Hey, Bonner. Who are you talking to," Patrick said weakly.

"A woman who says she is going to marry you."

Patrick turned his head to look who held his hand and said, "Beth has been with me for a long time, I think. If I'm hallucinating, don't let me wake up. I love you, Beth Formstone. If you're real or not. Be my wife."

Beth kissed him passionately and held onto his hand, afraid she might hurt his shoulder. "Does that answer your question. You'll never get away from me, ever again."

The two policemen, guarding the door, snapped to attention and greeted Judge Otis and Emma Webster.

"Patrick, how are you today?" Emma's Webster asked. "And who are you, miss?"

"I'm the girl who will marry Patrick as soon as he heals. Now, I'll stay here so he will never leave me."

"Aunt Emma, this is Beth Formstone. Beth, this is Judge Otis Webster and my Aunt Emma," Webster whispered.

"A wedding, how wonderful. Isn't it Otis? If you have no place to stay in Memphis, we have an extra bed. You can tell us all about yourself and Patrick, Otis performs marriages," said Emma.

Judge Webster looked at Beth and said, "Emma, for one time, I approve of your acting Cupid."

The doctors released Memphis detective Patrick McBride four days before Christmas. Bill Bonner and Albert Sidney Smith help McBride into his apartment. Beth Formstone supervised. She cleaned and arranged the apartment to make his recovery more comfortable. During Patrick's stay in the hospital, Beth stayed with Emma and the Judge. The two women planned a wedding the day after Christmas and Judge Webster agreed to officiate.

Beth moved into Patrick's apartment to care for him during his recovery. Millicent Blanchard came by his apartment and introduced herself.

"I fell in love with Patrick at the Top Hat Club when he rescued me from an embarrassing situation. If you ever decide to leave Patrick, I'll take him in a heartbeat."

"I think not. I thought I lost him for good, and I will never let Patrick McBride out of my sight," said Beth and told Millicent her story.

When Judge Webster asked Bill Bonner, the best man, for the wedding ring, Beth saw it for the first time and took in a deep breath.

Patrick nodded, and she understood that the colonel gave him the ring that belonged to Formstone's first wife. As was Colonel Formstone's wish, the ring bonded Beth and Patrick together.

Judge Otis and Emma Webster hosted a post-wedding party in their home. Judge Webster complained it had too many lawyers including Charles McMasters and Lydia, District Attorney Robert Ingraham and Memphis policemen David Flaherty, Bill Bonner, Albert Sidney Smith and others. The judge had to wait until the guests left to enjoy a glass of fine Scotch whiskey.

The End